Great Rail-Trails Series

THE OFFICIAL
RAILS-TO-
TRAILS
CONSERVANCY GUIDEBOOK

RAILS
–to–
TRAILS
CONSERVANCY

Washington
& Oregon

by
Mia Angela Barbera

The
Globe
Pequot
Press

Guilford, Connecticut

ABOUT THE AUTHOR

Mia Angela Barbera is passionate about play: riding, rolling, gliding, walking, and dancing. She believes that play keeps people healthy and happy. Mia shares her love of movement and outdoor exploration with her cross-country and downhill-ski, snowboard, and in-line skate students, her senior exercisers, and her ballroom dance friends. Mia is an exercise physiologist and social worker who finds outdoor exploration to be uplifting. It gets us out to meet new neighbors, gives us a sense of community, and never ceases to surprise us.

Copyright ©2001 by The Globe Pequot Press

Cover illustration: Rails-to-Trails Conservancy
Cover design: Laura Augustine
Text design: Lesley Weissman-Cook
Maps: Tim Kissel/Trailhead Graphics, Inc., copyright © The Globe Pequot Press
All photographs are by the author unless otherwise noted.

Library of Congress Cataloging-in-Publication Data
Barbera, Mia Angela.
  Rails-to-Trails. Washington, Oregon / by Mia Angela Barbera. — 1st ed.
    p. cm. — (Great rail-trails series)
    ISBN 0-7627-0696-1
    1. Rail-trails—Washington (State)—Guidebooks. 2. Rail-trails—Oregon—Guidebooks. 3. Outdoor recreation—Washington (State)—Guidebooks. 4. Outdoor recreation—Oregon—Guidebooks. 5. Washington (State)—Guidebooks. 6. Oregon—Guidebooks. I. Title. II. Great rail-trails series.

GV191.42.W2 B37 2001
917.9504'44—dc21   2001033701

Manufactured in the United States of America
First Edition/Third Printing

CONTENTS

Southwestern Washington's Top Rail-Trails

Eastern Washington's Top Rail-Trails

More Rail-Trails

OREGON

McClellan Butte forms a scenic backdrop for cyclists on the John Wayne Pioneer Trail.

T he rail-trails of Washington and Oregon provide scenic refuge, education, history, play, and body-beating adventure. Pick your trails and enjoy the surrounding cities, towns, and landscapes.

The trails I'll describe in these pages range from a 12-foot-wide paved path to a narrow, rugged, dirt single-track. You'll look out over an unobstructed view of the Columbia River, up to surrounding desert canyon walls, ahead through dense evergreen forest, or down upon neighborhood homes. Skaters, cyclists, equestrians, anglers, walkers, runners, skiers, snowshoers, and strollers join together to get fit, get relaxed, get together, or get to work in these linear parks. The trails skirt wineries, dams, cultural centers, waterfalls, old mines, rivers, lakes, fine dining, breweries, and the ocean.

A Bit of Pacific Northwest Rail History

The Pacific Northwest is separated east from west by the Cascade Mountains. Agriculture built the east, where you'll find distinct seasons and striking rock formations. Logging dominated the temperate western side, which features lush forests and interesting urban centers.

Before the railroad reached them, Washington and Oregon were islands, their geographic isolation restricting trade. The story of how the railroad got here fills volumes. Territorial and financial politics, bankruptcy, buyouts, personal glory, personal breakdown, and financial maneuvering paint as chaotic and colorful a picture as you'll find in any chunk of history.

Simply getting to the mountain passes in winter to scope out a railroad route left engineers fighting for their lives. Even after the tracks were built, traveling over passes, below rock cliffs, above rivers, and through tunnels put rail passengers at risk of smoke asphyxiation and avalanches of snow and rock. In fact, the worst disaster in railroad history played out on Stevens Pass in 1910. A heavy snowstorm stopped one train on the tracks. After the frightened passengers watched rockslides and collapsing trees for eight days, an avalanche shoved the railcars off the track into the valley below. Ninety-six people lost their lives.

In 1850 railroads were experimental; few lines in the country were more than 150 miles long. In 1851 the first tracks were set down in the Pacific Northwest—a crude 6-mile portage line built alongside the Cascades Rapids on the Washington side of the Columbia River. The train was not powered by an engine: Instead, the flatcars were hauled by mules. The first steam train arrived in 1862. By 1863, 19 miles of track had been laid in Oregon and 6 in Washington, all beside the Columbia River. Because the rapids were impassable by steamboats on this important inland water route, railroad portages picked up each load and dropped it off at a ship on the other side of the turbulent waters. The next set of tracks was built over the next decade to serve the agricultural Willamette Valley in Oregon.

In 1883 the first tracks reached the Pacific Northwest from the East; the dream of reaching the Pacific Coast had started decades earlier, however. In 1864 the U.S. Congress authorized the largest land grant in American history: A 60-million-acre swath the size of New England, extending from Lake Superior to the Pacific Ocean, was given to the Northern Pacific Railroad. Even when you subtract the land that the company forfeited by failing to meet deadlines, Northern Pacific netted 39 million acres from this deal—twice the

The Lake Wallula Scenic River Hiking Trail follows the rugged banks of the Columbia River in Oregon.

size of any other railroad grant. As a result, when many railroads consolidated into the Burlington Northern Railroad in 1970, this company became one of the largest private landholders in the country.

Northern Pacific's land grant provided it with timber to build tracks and cash from land sales. Land sales adjacent to the railroad path served another purpose. While eastern railroads were built between existing towns and transportation centers, this line would—in the words of one cynic—"have to generate passengers and freight revenue by running from nowhere in particular to nowhere at all, through thousands of miles of rugged and lightly populated country." The railroads of the West, in other words, would have to foster development. The area had no investors or capital; only the federal government could finance this project. The railroad would have to build the need for trains.

Due to financial problems, the Oregon Railway and Navigation Company (ORN) reached Portland from the East before the Northern Pacific route to Tacoma became a reality. In 1883 the owner of the ORN, Henry Villard, purchased the Northern Pacific to extend the ORN tracks east from the Columbia Gorge. He consolidated the two railroad companies to build the first railroad to connect the Midwest with the Pacific Northwest. Northern Pacific tracks had reached Tacoma from Portland years before, completing a route to Washington State. Only when threatened by a Seattle businessmen's plan to build a line to the lucrative agricultural valleys of the Palouse and Walla Walla did Henry Villard extend his railroad up through the Yakima Valley, over Stampede Pass and into Tacoma. In 1893 the Northern Pacific went bankrupt, and in January of that year the next transcontinental line reached over Stevens Pass and into Seattle.

The railroad did build the need for trains. Wherever a depot sprouted, so did a post office and a population. Between 1887 and 1889, 95,000 newcomers arrived in Washington, a number of people equal to the residents of the territory in 1880. Seattle's population grew from 3,533 in 1880 to 42,837 in 1890. Tacoma went from 1,098 to 36,006. Many towns along the railroad line in rural Washington had a larger population than they have today.

It was not until 1909 that a third set of tracks hit Seattle. The Chicago, Milwaukee & St. Paul Railway did not make instant railroad history when it arrived in the Pacific Northwest, as the first two lines had. A more significant event came in 1917, however, when the Milwaukee Road became the first electrified transcontinental railroad and the nation's longest electrified train. Travel became easier, faster, cheaper, and safer. Not only did the electrical system help clear smoke from railway tunnels, but trains braking while heading downhill regenerated power back into the overhead catenary wires—thereby powering the uphill trains. The electric was so well designed that it operated from 1917 into the 1970s with few problems.

Trains of the Pacific Northwest carried passengers to a weekend at the shore, or on an elegant ride from town to town. Trains laden with logs climbed switchbacks to reach the mills or ships departing for the Orient. Coal cars ran to the bunkers on Puget Sound to ship their load to San Francisco. Produce from the fertile soils of the Palouse, Walla Walla, and Willamette Valleys, as well as southeastern King County, rolled through farmland to warehouses and on to the cities.

Today these same railbeds allow you to journey for days through neighborhoods and on isolated pathways, resting at hotels, bed-and-breakfasts, or campsites. You'll see the farmland, the mines, and the trees that built the Pacific Northwest once the rail lines freed the area from geographic isolation. The trails now free us to see our community, our industries, and our neighbor's way of life—traveling from town to town, desert to mountains, city to sea; beside huge rivers, forest streams, urban lakes, Puget Sound, and the Pacific Ocean. Stay the weekend or spend a week on these trails, enjoying the culture and beauty of the Pacific Northwest.

Benefits of Rail-Trails

Railbeds are an ideal location for trails. They come in all sizes, surfaces, and steepnesses. The paths of main lines are quite flat with wide, rounded turns, allowing them to safely accommodate equestrians, beginner skaters and cyclists, cross-country skiers, snowshoers, and families. Main lines rarely exceed a 2 percent grade, even on mountain switchbacks. Logging lines occasionally offer steeper grades for a challenging mountain bike ride or a great workout on foot.

Biking the Big Brother and Little Brother trestles of the King County Interurban Trail.

Rail-trails provide an ideal transportation corridor for commuters. Many lie in the path of local industry or run from rural areas to city centers. They often link to bus routes and highways. Get creative. Take a bus halfway to work and ride or walk the rest of the route, or bus to work and bicycle home. Try a rail-trail on the Cascade Bicycle Club's Seattle Bike to Work Day and get free snacks and souvenirs as a bonus.

Much like the logging roads of the Pacific Northwest, however, rail-trails also frequently abandon streets and highways for a more remote experience. They're parks that go somewhere. They expose us to our neighbors, to diverse lifestyles and commercial areas, to rural diners and waterfront restaurants, and, of course, past many espresso stands. They bring our community closer together and provide the best of tourist opportunities.

Locals along the rail-trails of Washington and Oregon claim that they became more active after the trails were built. One lovely young woman from Algona, Washington, reported, "I lost weight after my baby was born by walking this trail every day." Her friend added, enthusiastically, "Did you know this used to be a railroad line?" Such conversations with strangers rarely happen on the street. They're common on the trails.

This waterfall can be seen near the Red Town Trailhead on the Coal Creek Park Trail.

One of the great joys of train travel lies in the route—one moment you're in the middle of the city, and the next you're in a remote region of beauty. That we can now enjoy such experiences on a rail-trail is nothing less than a gift from the railroad companies and our cities, counties, states, the federal government, community advocates, and the Rails-to-Trails Conservancy.

The History of the Rails-to-Trails Conservancy

As road construction and increased reliance on cars forced railroads to the sidelines, the question arose: What to do with all the abandoned tracks that crisscrossed the state?

Enter the Rails-to-Trails Conservancy, an environmental group that since 1986 has campaigned to convert the railroad tracks to nature paths.

The beauty of the Rails-to-Trails Conservancy (RTC) is that by converting the railroad rights-of-way to public use, it has not only preserved a part of our nation's history, but allows a variety of outdoor enthusiasts to enjoy the paths and trails.

Bicyclists, in-line skaters, nature lovers, hikers, equestrians, and cross-country skiers can enjoy rail-trails, as can railroad history buffs. There is truly something for everyone on these trails, many of which are also wheelchair accessible.

The concept of preserving these valuable corridors and converting them into multiuse public trails began in the Midwest, where railroad abandonments were most widespread. Once the tracks came out, people started using the corridors for walking and hiking while exploring the railroad relics that were left along the rail beds, including train stations, mills, trestles, bridges, and tunnels.

Although it was easy to convince people that the rails-to-trails concept was worthwhile, the reality of actually converting abandoned railroad corridors into public trails proved a great challenge. From the late 1960s until the early 1980s, many rail-trail efforts failed as corridors were lost to development, sold to the highest bidder, or broken into many pieces.

In 1983, Congress enacted an amendment to the National Trails System Act directing the Interstate Commerce Commission to allow about-to-be abandoned railroad lines to be "railbanked," or set aside for future transportation use while being used as trails in the interim. In essence, this law preempts rail corridor abandonment, keeping the corridors intact as trails or for other transportation uses into the future.

This powerful new piece of legislation made it easier for public and private agencies and organizations to acquire rail corridors for trails, but many projects still failed because of short deadlines, lack of information, and local opposition.

In 1986, the Rails-to-Trails Conservancy was formed to provide a national voice for the creation of rail-trails. The RTC quickly developed a strategy that was designed to preserve the largest amount of rail corridor in the shortest period of time. A national advocacy program was formed to defend the new railbanking law in the courts and in Congress; this was coupled with a direct project-assistance program to help public agencies and local rail-trail groups overcome the challenges of converting a rail into a trail.

The strategy is working. In 1986, the Rails-to-Trails Conservancy knew of only seventy-five rail-trails in the United States, and ninety projects in the works. Today there are more than a thousand rail-trails on the ground and many more projects underway. The RTC vision of creating an interconnected network of trails across the country is becoming a reality.

The thriving rails-to-trails movement has created more than 10,000 miles of public trails for a wide range of users. People across the country are now realizing the incredible benefits of the rail-trails.

How to Get Involved

If you really enjoy rail-trails, there are opportunities to join the movement to save abandoned rail corridors and to create more trails. Donating even a small amount of your time can help get more trails up and going. Here are some ways you can help the effort:

- Write a letter to your city, county, or state elected official in favor of pro-trail legislation. You can also write a letter to the editor of your local newspaper highlighting a trail or trail project.
- Attend a public hearing to voice support for a local trail.
- Volunteer to plant flowers or trees along an existing trail or to spend several hours helping a cleanup crew on a nearby rail-trail project.
- Lead a hike along an abandoned corridor with your friends or a community group.
- Become an active member of a trail effort in your area. Many groups host trail events, undertake fund-raising campaigns, publish brochures and newsletters, and carry out other activities to promote a trail or project. Virtually all of these efforts are organized and staffed by volunteers and there is always room for another helping hand.

Whatever your time allows, get involved. The success of a community's rail-trail depends on the level of citizen participation. The Rails-to-Trails Conservancy enjoys local and national support. By joining the RTC you will get discounts on all of its publications and merchandise while supporting the largest national trails organization in the United States. To become a member, use the order form at the back of the book.

How to Use Rail-Trails

By design, rail-trails accommodate a variety of trail users. While this is generally one of the many benefits of rail-trails, it also can lead to occasional conflicts among trail users. Everyone should take responsibility to ensure trail safety by following a few simple trail etiquette guidelines.

One of the most basic etiquette rules is "Wheels yield to heels." The figure below indicates the correct protocol for yielding right-of-way. Bicyclists (and in-line skaters) yield to other users; pedestrians yield to equestrians.

Generally, this means that you need to warn the users to whom you are yielding of your presence. If, as a bicyclist, you fail to warn a walker that you are about to pass, the walker could step in front of you, causing an accident that easily could have been prevented. Similarly, it is best to slow down and warn a equestrian of your presence. A horse can be startled by a bicycle, so make verbal contact with the rider and be sure it is safe to pass.

Here are some other guidelines you should follow to promote trail safety:

- Obey all trail rules posted at trailheads.
- Stay to the right except when passing.
- Pass slower traffic on the left; yield to oncoming traffic when passing.
- Give a clear warning signal when passing.
- Always look ahead and behind when passing.
- Travel at a responsible speed.
- Keep pets on a leash.
- Do not trespass on private property.
- Move off the trail surface when stopped to allow other users to pass.
- Yield to other trail users when entering and crossing the trail.
- Do not disturb the wildlife.
- Do not swim in areas not designated for swimming.
- Watch out for traffic when crossing the street.
- Obey all traffic signals.

The Morse Creek Trestle of the Olympic Discovery Trail.

How to Use This Book

For this book I've chosen Washington and Oregon's top rail-trails based on length, historical or aesthetic features, access, and location. I also found that some trails benefit from a more detailed description; shorter trails are listed under More Rail-Trails, because a brief summary is all you need to locate and enjoy them.

At the beginning of each chapter, you will find a map showing the location of the rail-trails within that region. The main rail-trails featured in this book include basic maps for your convenience. It is recommended, however, that street maps, topographic maps such as USGS quads, or a state atlas be used to supplement the maps in this book. The text description of every trail begins with the following information:

- **Trail name:** The official name of the rail-trail.
- **Activities:** A list of icons tells you what kinds of activities are appropriate for each trail.
- **Location:** The areas through which the trail passes.
- **Length:** The length of the trail, including how many miles are currently open and, for those trails that are built on partially abandoned corridors, the number of miles actually on the rail line.
- **Surface:** The materials that make up the rail-trail vary from trail

to trail. This section describes each trail's surface. Materials range from asphalt and crushed stone to the significantly more rugged original railroad ballast.

- **Wheelchair access:** Some of the rail-trails are wheelchair accessible. This allows physically challenged individuals the opportunity to explore the rail-trails with family and friends.
- **Difficulty:** The rail-trails range from very easy to hard, depending on the grade of the trail and the general condition of the trail.
- **Food:** The book will indicate the names of the towns near the rail-trails in which restaurants and fast-food shops are located.
- **Rest rooms:** If a rest room is available near the trail, the book will provide you with its location.
- **Seasons:** Most of these trails are open year-round, but special circumstances, such as severe winter rains or localized flooding, may preclude the use of certain routes during some seasons.
- **Access and parking:** The book will provide you with directions to the rail-trails and describe parking availability.
- **Rentals:** Some of the rail-trails have bicycle shops and skating stores nearby. This will help you locate bike or skate rentals, or a shop in which you can have repairs made if you have problems with your equipment.
- **Contact:** The name and contact information for each trail manager is listed here. The selected contacts are generally responsible for managing the trail and can provide additional information about the trail and its condition.
- **Bus route:** Bus routes listed provide an alternate return route for individuals traveling the trails one way. Some extend the entire length of the trail, others cover only a portion. Contact carriers directly for more detailed and up-to-date information.
- **Description:** The major rail-trails include an overview of the trail and its history, followed by a mile-by-mile description, allowing you the chance to anticipate the experience of the trail.

Key to Activities Icons

Backpacking

Bird-watching

Camping

Cross-country skiing

Fishing

Historic Sites

Horseback Riding

In-line Skating

Mountain Biking

Paddlesports

Road Bicycling

Running

Swimming

Walking/Day Hiking

Wildlife Viewing

Snowshoeing

Key to Map Icons

P Parking

I Information

Rest Rooms

R Rentals

A Camping

Note: All map scales are approximate.

Rails-to-Trails

WASHINGTON

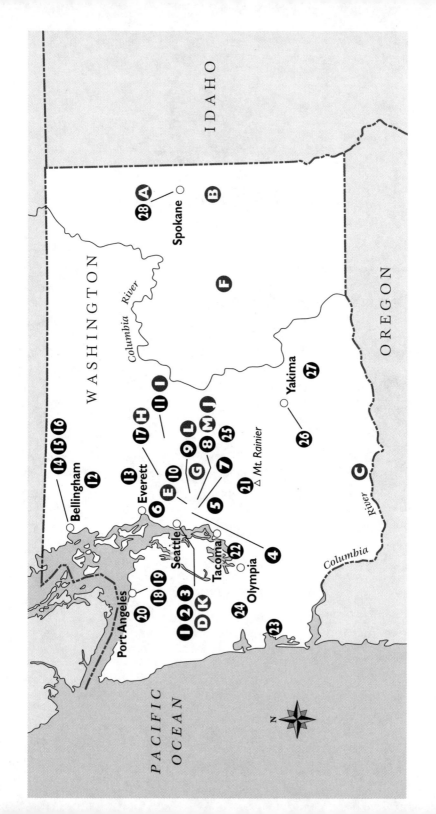

Washington
Puget Sound

1. Burke-Gilman Trail
2. Seattle Waterfront Pathway
3. Elliott Bay Trail
4. Coal Creek Park Trail
5. King County Interurban Trail
6. Snohomish County Interurban Trail
7. Cedar River Trail and Lake Wilderness Trail
8. Tiger Mountain State Forest
9. Preston-Snoqualmie Trail
10. Snoqualmie Valley Trail and Snoqualmie Valley Trail Extension

Northwestern Washington

11. Iron Goat Trail
12. Cascade Trail
13. Snohomish County Centennial Trail
14. Whatcom County and Bellingham Interurban Trail
15. South Bay Trail
16. Railroad Trail
17. Wallace Falls Railway Trail
18. Olympic Discovery Trail: Morse Creek to Siebert Creek
19. Olympic Discovery Trail: Port Angeles Waterfront
20. Spruce Railroad Trail

Southwestern Washington

21. Foothills Trail
22. Chehalis Western Trail (Woodard Bay Trail)
23. Chehalis Trail (Raymond to South Bend Riverfront Trail)
24. Lake Sylvia State Park

Eastern Washington

25. John Wayne Pioneer Trail (West)
26. Cowiche Canyon Trail
27. Lower Yakima Valley Pathway
28. Spokane River Centennial Trail

More Washington Rail-Trails

A. Ben Burr Trail
B. Colfax Trail
C. Dry Creek Trail
D. Duwamish Bikeway
E. Issaquah-Preston Trail
F. John Wayne Pioneer Trail—Milwaukee Road Corridor
G. Middle Fork Trail
H. Necklace Valley Trail
I. Pacific Crest National Scenic Trail, Stevens Pass Right-of-Way Section
J. Rainier Multiuse Trail
K. Ship Canal Trail
L. Snoqualmie Centennial Trail
M. West Tiger Railroad Grade

INTRODUCTION

Washington State boasts more than fifty rail-trails. The state, its cities, towns, and citizen groups deserve mountains of praise for their hard work in overcoming the financial, political, and social obstacles in their way as they developed these paths to fitness, sensible transportation, and joy.

The trails of Puget Sound run on main lines that once carried timber, coal, and passengers, logging lines that headed into the hills, and elegant interurban trolleys. The Burke-Gilman Trail receives the heaviest use. Commuters, cyclists, skaters, children, and walkers have all discovered that there's no better route for exploring the north-side neighborhoods of Seattle. Take yourself to breakfast, lunch, and dinner on this route. Sip cappuccino on the Ship Canal, watch floatplanes land while you enjoy happy hour beside Lake Washington, watch kites soar over Lake Union; ride, walk, or skate through the U-district at the University of Washington and finish with an outdoor movie or the Sunday market in Fremont. Daniel Burke and Judge Thomas Gilman, founding fathers of Seattle, built the Seattle, Lakeshore & Eastern Railroad on this route.

The Elliot Bay Trail and the Seattle Waterfront Pathway carve a corridor through the downtown waterfront and through parks, ending at Smith Cove Park and Marina, former site of coal bunkers.

The King County Interurban Trail heads through the industrial regions and neighborhoods of South King County, past the racetrack and a huge mall to the tiny towns of Algona and Pacific. Commute, shop, have a day at the races, tour the cities along the way, or just enjoy a great workout while on this wide, paved trail. Urban trails also head north from Lynnwood to Everett along the old trolley line.

The trails east of Seattle offer some screaming mountain bike rides in Tiger Mountain State Forest, a ravine built from coal tailings, a great commuter trail along the Cedar River, and a 36-mile trail through the Snoqualmie Valley. The Cedar River Trail starts in the city of Renton on Lake Washington and ends on a wooded riverside pathway, enjoyed by equestrians. The Snoqualmie Valley Trail traverses the rolling terrain of a rural area showing the signs of development. Local antiques shops and eateries remain while Starbucks, grocery chains, and fast foods encroach. This is a pretty valley that takes you near Snoqualmie Falls with the luxurious Salish Lodge at its lip. The nearby Snoqualmie Centennial Trail begins at the Northwest Railroad Museum and continues alongside the old tracks, crowded with engines from the past. The Snoqualmie Valley Trail presently connects to the John Wayne Pioneer Trail. The gentle beauty of the Snoqualmie and Snohomish Valleys will be even more accessible when the Snoqualmie Valley Trail connects to the Snohomish Centennial Trail in northwestern Washington, creating an exceptional, continuous regional trail system.

Rail-trails in northwestern Washington pass by farms, through forests, beside waterfalls, through the college town of Bellingham, and out to the Olympic Peninsula. Enjoy the calm waters of Lake Crescent and the views of distant peaks from the Spruce Railroad Trail. Enjoy the oceanfront city of Port Angeles and the forest bouquets of wildflowers on the two completed sections of the Olympic Discovery Trail. The Wallace Falls Railway Trail climbs through the forest for a good look at a logging route ascended by the "steam donkey" trains, along with some dramatic waterfalls. The Iron Goat Trail to Stevens Pass is an impressive interpretive hiking trail that transports you back to the difficulties and disasters that the Great Northern Railroad experienced as it made its way through this rugged territory.

Southwestern Washington offers several rural rail-trails. To the east you'll find the Foothills Trail, in the shadow of Mount Rainier; to the west is the Chehalis Trail on the Willapa River. Follow the trail to Raymond from South Bend, discovering this Oyster Capital of the World. There's also an easily accessible refuge just off I–5 near the state capital of Olympia (Chehalis Western Trail) and rugged dirt trails in Lake Sylvia State Park.

Head to eastern Washington to find sunshine and hot, dry desert. East of the Cascades you'll discover Yakima wine country, the pretty Cowiche

Canyon, and a trail through the city of Spokane to the Idaho border. Turbulent dams, museums, a century-old merry-go-round, and an equestrian area accent the 37-mile Spokane River Centennial Trail. Follow 113 miles of the path of the *Olympian-Hiawatha* passenger train that once rolled from Seattle to Chicago on the Milwaukee Road. Travel through changes in terrain, climate, and scenery, along rivers, through towns, past a unique espresso shop and cafe, and to the edge of the Columbia River on the John Wayne Pioneer Trail. A 2.25-mile tunnel through a mountain pass is dark and eerie and fun to explore. Adventurous travelers can continue east to the border of Idaho on the undeveloped portion of the trail.

Seattle and many surrounding areas have a serious traffic problem: The problem is us. Commuting on a rail-trail is just as sensible as was commuting on the trains that ran these routes—and just as pleasant. Hop a bus one way or for part of your route and take your bike, skates, or your feet the rest of the way. Get fit and lean, meet people, protect the environment, and live longer. Men and women in their eighties and nineties haul groceries on primitive bikes in countries like Italy, Denmark, and China. We can likewise mount our modern bikes and ride to work in comfort as we age healthy and feisty. The Cascade Bicycle Club honors one such commuter each month and can help you get started. Check the bus, talk to your coworkers, and make a plan. And join the Cascade Bicycle Club's Bike to Work Day this summer. (See Appendix B for contact information.)

Wherever or however you start your tour, don't miss the chance to see, play, study, commute, or simply wander Washington's wonderful rail-trails.

Washington's

TOP RAIL-TRAILS

 Burke–Gilman Trail

Seattle's popular Burke–Gilman Trail invites you on a tour of funky Fremont, Lake Union and the ship canal, the University District, Lake Washington, and north-end neighborhoods. You'll pass above the old Sand Point naval base and along the busy, commercial Lake City Way as well as a cornucopia of tempting eateries.

Activities:

Location: North Seattle to Lake Forest Park, King County

Length: 14 miles

Surface: Paved

Wheelchair access: The entire trail is wheelchair accessible.

Difficulty: Easy

Food: In the town of Fremont and along Lake City Way, you'll find everything from breweries and grocery stores to fast food and gourmet dining.

Rest rooms: You'll find rest room facilities at Gas Works Park, Burke-Gilman Place Park, Mathews Beach Park, and Tracy Owen Station, as well as various commercial establishments near the trail. There are also water fountains along the way.

Seasons: The trail can be used year-round.

Access and parking: You can access the trail from many points. The southern end of the trail sits at Eighth Avenue Northwest and Northwest 43rd Street just off Leary Way. Park on the street and hop on the trail at Hales Brewery. Gas Works Park, which offers parking and picnic facilities, is on Northeast Northlake Way, just south of Fremont. Mathews Beach Park (with parking, picnicking, and swimming) is 7 miles north. To get there, take Sand Point Way Northeast to Northeast 93rd Street, then turn east, toward Lake Washington.

Tracy Owen Station is the trail's northern terminus and offers parking, picnicking, and fishing. It's found on 61st Avenue Northeast and Northeast Bothell Way in Kenmore. The trail continues 15 miles to Marymoor Park in Redmond as the Sammamish River Trail.

You can also park along the road in many areas, including Fremont Canal Park, found at Phinney Avenue North and Leary Way Northwest.

Rentals: You can rent in-line skates at Urban Surf, across from Gas Works Park at 2100 North Northlake Way; (206) 545–9463. For bicycles, visit The Bicycle Center at 4529 Sand Point Way; (206) 523–8300.

Contact: City of Seattle Transportation Bicycle & Pedestrian Program, (206) 684–7583, www.ci.seattle.wa.us/td/bgtrail.asp

Bus routes: #372, #312, or #307. For more information, call Metro Transit at (206) 553–3000. Or visit the Web site at transit.metrokc.gov

• •

W hat a train ride this must have been! In 1885 Judge Thomas Burke and Daniel Gilman, two of Seattle's city fathers, set out to establish the Seattle, Lakeshore & Eastern Railroad. Originally planned to connect with the Canadian Transcontinental at Sumas, the rail line made it only to Arlington. Still, it became a major regional line serving Puget Sound logging areas. Northern Pacific purchased the line in 1913, used it heavily until 1963, and finally abandoned it in 1971. A cooperative effort by King County, Seattle, and the University of Washington then led to the right-of-way's development as a trail, dedicated in 1978.

Now a heavily used recreation and commuter pathway, the Burke-Gilman Trail takes you past boats, bridges, and breweries. You can stop at cafes, parks, and bookstores while marveling at the 72,500 seats of Husky Stadium, the Gothic architecture of the University of Washington, and the shiny, square buildings that have been added in recent years.

Be alert if you travel this trail on a sunny day or warm evening: Oodles of baby strollers, commuters, cyclists, skaters, and walkers will be right there with you. Be cautious and considerate.

The trail is described here from its southern terminus at Hales Brewery to the northern trailhead at Tracy Owen Station, but it can be accessed from many points along the way.

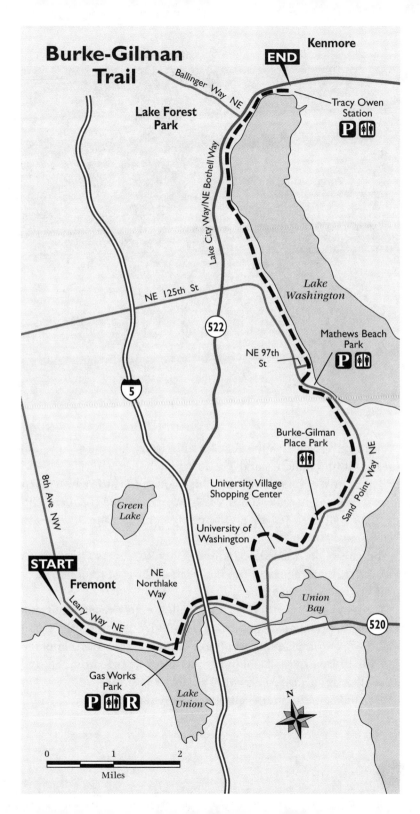

Burke-Gilman Trail

Kenmore

END

Ballinger Way NE

Tracy Owen
Station

Lake Forest
Park

Lake City Way/NE Bothell Way

Lake
Washington

NE 125th St

522

Mathews Beach
Park

NE 97th
St

Burke-Gilman
Place Park

5

Sand Point Way NE

University Village
Shopping Center

Green
Lake

University of
Washington

START

Fremont

NE
Northlake
Way

Union
Bay

8th Ave NW

Leary Way NE

520

Gas Works
Park

Lake
Union

N

0   1   2
Miles

A cyclist in Tracy Owen Station.

Fremont Canal Park lies just 0.5 mile from the trail's beginning; here you'll find benches and a waterfront shelter with tile artwork. Peek at Ponti's across the canal: This is one of Seattle's best Italian seafood restaurants. The Red Hook Brewery is on the corner of Phinney. The trail then leaves Fremont city center to dip down to the edge of Lake Union.

You can make a side trip here to enjoy Fremont's street art and food, the "neon bridge lady," and the sign declaring Fremont the center of the known universe.

The trail passes Gas Works Park at mile 1.8; there's an uphill grade here. Stop for great views of the city, Mount Rainier, and Lake Union. Read the historic plaque posted on a bridge pillar as you approach the "Wall of Death" (a bright orange motorcycle velodrome) at mile 3. You'll cross several roads over the next 4 miles. As you pass University Hospital, the south campus, and Husky Stadium at 3.6 miles, a sign directs you to the Lake Washington Loop. You are on the northern section of this loop. The sign points you to the southern section, which follows city streets around the south end of Lake Washington. Note the contrast here between the pointed tops of the University's stone architecture and the glass rectangles of the modern buildings. Arrive at 25th Avenue Northeast and the University Village Shopping Center at 5 miles. There are lots of treats and espresso to be discovered here.

The trail from here north is easy; it's especially good for beginner skaters and bikers. You'll find just a bit of grade, one wooden bridge crossing, and mostly small street crossings. A jogging path takes you as far as Lakeside Place Northeast.

At 40th Avenue Northeast you'll pass a grocery store and Burke-Gilman Place Park with picnic tables and rest rooms, then enter a forested area. Benches are placed here and there for the next few miles. Maples, dogwoods, and trimmed hedges frame lake views north of Northeast 77th Street (mile 8). There's a fairly smooth trail surface with a slight grade and frequent small road crossings. A bridge crosses Sand Point Way to Mathews Beach Park at 9 miles. This lakeside park has swings, a play area, picnicking, and swimming. North of Northeast 97th Street, the character of the trail changes once again. Waterfront homes are sandwiched together much like the narrow streets of a European city; the small, sharp angles of gingerbread houses and brick Tudors offer an interesting contrast with modern square homes. Pass Lakeside Place Northeast at 10.6 miles. Northeast 153rd Street has parking for three cars. The trail reaches Lake City Way at Northeast Ballinger Way (mile 13.5). Take a drink of water from the serpent here.

Great eats and treats appear all along the remainder of the trail. The Lake Forest Town Center brings the city to the 'burbs with Honey Bear Bakery, 3rd Place Books, and a small food circus. You may walk in on one of the bookstore's events. You may also be drawn to the bakery's 6-inch-tall slice of Basque cake, tiramisu with fruit, and more cakes, cakes, cakes. Quiches, salads, and vegan fare accompany the monster cakes. Even if you manage to bypass these temptations, a Starbucks and an ice cream store are around the corner.

Cliffords is one of the restaurants along the trail boasting great lake views.

You don't need to leave the trail for entertainment. A small grassy park with water and rest rooms sits 0.5 mile from Town Center on the trail. Just ahead and above the trail lies Cliffords. View float-planes from this restaurant's cozy tavern and deck while you enjoy afternoon appetizers.

Java Louie's (with milk shakes and espresso), Tully's, Starbucks, and Mia Roma's join the fast-food spots on the main drag ahead. The Burke-Gilman Trail officially ends at Tracy Owen Station in Kenmore, although you can continue traveling to Marymoor Park from here on the Sammamish River Trail. Hop a bus to return to your starting point: The #372 will take you back to the University District.

This pathway and the connected Elliott Bay Trail (Trail 3) provide a scenic tour of the downtown Seattle waterfront. Park the car, grab your bike, skates, or walking shoes, and head for the water. The trail runs through a lively tourist area, past the ferry docks, along a trolley line, and adjacent to Safeco Field.

Activities:

Location: Downtown Seattle, King County

Length: 2 miles

Surface: Paved

Wheelchair access: The entire trail is wheelchair accessible.

Difficulty: Easy

Food: There are many restaurants and fast-food places along the waterfront.

Rest rooms: Rest rooms and drinking water are available at Myrtle Edwards Park.

Seasons: The trail can be used year-round.

Access and parking: To reach the Seattle Waterfront Pathway, head west from I–5 to Alaskan Way; the trail runs along Alaskan Way from South Royal Brougham Way (its southern end) to Broad Street (the northern terminus). You can access the trail anywhere along its length. Metered parking is available on streets. Myrtle Edwards Park, at the trail's northern end, also offers parking; it's metered until 6:00 P.M. except Saturday and holidays.

Rentals: Bikes can be rented from Blazing Saddles (1230 Western Avenue; 206–341–9994) at the base of Harborview near the Seattle Art Museum. You can rent both skates and bikes at Alpine Hut (2215 15th Avenue Northwest; 206–284–3575) near the Magnolia Bridge.

Contact: City of Seattle Transportation Bicycle and Pedestrian Program, (206) 684–7583.

Bus route: Seattle Waterfront Trolley

• • • • • • • • • • • • • • • • • • •

Tour the heart of the bustling Seattle waterfront on this lively urban pathway. The 8- to 10-foot-wide trail runs mostly along the east side of Alaskan Way; it shifts to the west between Cedar and

Broad Streets, near its northern end. Pedestrians can use either the sidewalk on the west side of Alaskan Way or this trail, as can bikers and skaters. The trail is a better choice if you're on wheels, however. Plan to go slowly and to stop and start and yield to pedestrians. Experienced cyclists may opt to ride the roadway.

This description runs from south to north, but you can access the trail anywhere along its length. As you embark from South Royal Brougham Way, grab a peek at Safeco Field. The sports arena features a retractable roof that alternately protects fans from rain and welcomes the sun into the game. (The Seattle Mariners' former venue, the Kingdome, was destroyed in 2000 when this controversial multi-million dollar stadium opened.) You'll then pass the ferry terminals and the aquarium as you head north and enjoy casual outdoor eating on the waterfront.

Look back when you're about 0.5 mile north of the ferry terminal to see the active tracks of the Burlington Northern Santa Fe Railway disappear into a tunnel beneath the city. The trolley now runs on what once were the Seattle, Lakeshore & Eastern tracks, which

The Seattle Waterfront Trolley runs parallel to the Pathway.

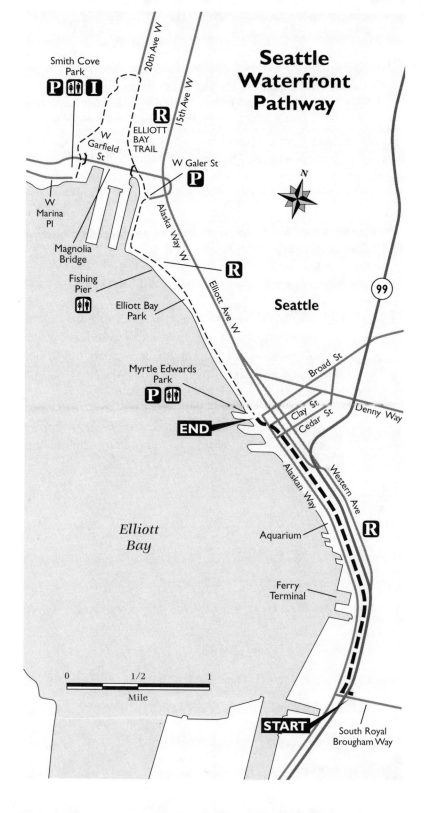

Seattle
Waterfront
Pathway

20th Ave W

15th Ave W

Smith Cove
Park

P 👥 **I**

R
ELLIOTT
BAY
TRAIL

W
Garfield
St

W Galer St
P

W
Marina
Pl

Alaska Way W

Magnolia
Bridge

Fishing
Pier
👥

Elliott Bay
Park

Elliott Ave W

R

Seattle

N

99

Myrtle Edwards
Park
P 👥

Broad St

Clay St.

Cedar St

Denny Way

END

Alaskan Way

Western Ave

Aquarium

R

*Elliott
Bay*

Ferry
Terminal

0   1/2   1
Mile

START

South Royal
Brougham Way

were purchased by the Northern Pacific Railroad Company. You can hop the trolley every 2 blocks for a rolling view of the activity.

If you're on foot, you might want to make a detour up the Pike Place Hillclimb at Pike Street to the market, shops, and more restaurants and activities. Stop to catch a peek at one of Pike Place Market's most popular attractions: fish vendors in white aprons hawking their wares by tossing them back and forth in a verbose game of catch. The tasty treats you can create with a crumpet at the Crumpet Shop are marvelous.

Shift to the west side of the street from Cedar to Broad Streets. If you'd like to combine this trip with the Elliott Bay Trail, which takes you farther north, just continue straight into the Myrtle Edwards parking lot. Whenever you're ready, turn around and return the way you came.

Cyclists may also want to extend this trip southward from Royal Brougham on Alaskan Way. Pedal this street south to Spokane Street, then turn right on Spokane to cross the lower West Seattle Bridge. This will connect you with the Duwamish and Alki Trails and the beach, bakeries, restaurants, and cafes at Alki Point.

Expect a disruption toward the southern end of this trail as Alaskan Way is ripped up and rebuilt over the next several years. A trail extension south to Atlantic Street will be included in this renovation.

The Elliott Bay Trail provides a picturesque tour of Seattle's downtown waterfront. It connects with the Seattle Waterfront Pathway (Trail 2) for a longer stroll or ride along the waterfront.

Activities:

Location: Downtown Seattle, King County

Length: 3.35 miles

Surface: Paved

Wheelchair access: The entire trail is wheelchair accessible.

Difficulty: Mostly easy, although the pavement may be bumpy for novice skaters and bikers. There are a few little hills and one short, narrow, steep hill.

Food: Numerous restaurants abut the Myrtle Edwards parking lot. The Happy Hooker at the Fishing Pier sells chips, candy, and soda. Restaurants at Smith Cove Marina include Palisades, an elegant place with a terrific Sunday brunch, a sushi spot, and a casual restaurant.

Rest rooms: There are rest rooms and water at Myrtle Edwards Park and the Fishing Pier. You'll also find rest rooms at Smith Cove Park.

Seasons: The trail can be used year-round. Smith Cove Park is open from 6:00 A.M. to 9:00 P.M. in summer, and 6:00 A.M. to 7:00 P.M. in winter. Both gates (under Magnolia Bridge and at 20th Street) are locked at dusk. Don't get trapped between them when they close!

Access and parking: To reach the Elliott Bay Trail, head west from I–5 to Alaskan Way. You can park at Myrtle Edwards Park (this trail's southern terminus), found at Alaskan Way and Broad Street. The lot here is metered until 6:00 P.M. except Saturday and holidays.

You can also park on West Galer Street—a good spot if the Myrtle Edwards lot is full or if you'd rather park for free. Continue north on Alaskan Way; after the Magnolia Bridge, the street name changes to 15th Avenue West. Turn west onto West Galer Street 1.3 miles north of the corner of Western and Denny, and park where Galer ends along the water.

Another option is to begin your tour at Smith Cove Park, at the trail's northern end; this will allow novice skaters and bikers to avoid a steep, narrow overpass and a railroad crossing. To reach the park, turn west onto West Galer Street from 15th Avenue West, cross the Magnolia Bridge, and continue to the Smith Cove Park exit.

Rentals: Bikes can be rented from Blazing Saddles (1230 Western Avenue; 206-341-9994) at the base of Harborview near the Seattle Art Museum. You can rent both skates and bikes at Alpine Hut (2215 15th Avenue Northwest; 206-284-3575) near the Magnolia Bridge.

Contact: City of Seattle Transportation Bicycle and Pedestrian Program, (206) 684-7583.

Bus routes: #15, #18. For more information call Metro Transit at (206) 553-3000. Or try the Web site at transit.metrokc.gov.

· ·

The Elliott Bay Trail winds through two contiguous parks as it passes between the waterfront and the active Burlington Northern Santa Fe Railroad line. The trail can be accessed from many points along the way; this description begins at Myrtle Edwards Park and continues north to Smith Cove. Starting from Myrtle Edwards, the trail is separated into different sections for wheels and for pedestrians. The wheels side is plagued with buckling pavement—a problem for beginners. Both trails are narrow but picturesque.

Visit the rose garden at 0.55 mile or work your way through the par course while you watch the activity on the sound. Sunsets can be spectacular here. At mile 1, you may want to stop at the Happy Hooker by the Fishing Pier for a candy bar or a soda; you'll also find rest rooms and drinking water. You'll reach the Galer Street parking area at 1.35 miles. Cross in front of the entrance to terminal 91 and turn left on the sidewalk to pass under the Magnolia Bridge. (Note: At press time plans were under way to re-route this final section of the trail and make it a direct waterfront route.)

As it leaves the waterfront beyond Galer Street, the trail becomes bumpy. It crosses old railroad tracks, quickly and briefly becomes very narrow, then climbs and descends a steep overpass. Cyclists and pedestrians, beware of skaters: They have less control than you, and need more room. Beyond this overpass, however, the trail is flat and wide.

Several popular bike routes take off from 20th Avenue West at mile 1.68 (0.8 mile beyond Galer Street), including trips to the Chittenden Locks or to Fremont (see Trail 1 for more information on the funky town of Fremont). After 20th Avenue, the trail curves around a huge parking lot, where cars are delivered from overseas. Cross

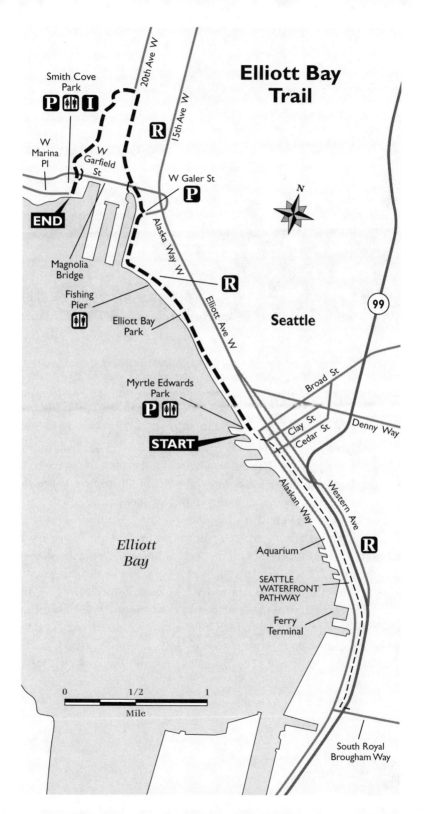

Elliott Bay Trail

Smith Cove Park

20th Ave W

15th Ave W

R

W Marina Pl

W Garfield St

W Galer St

P

END

Alaska Way W

Magnolia Bridge

Fishing Pier

Elliott Bay Park

Elliott Ave W

R

Seattle

99

Myrtle Edwards Park

P

START

Broad St

Clay St

Cedar St

Denny Way

Alaskan Way

Western Ave

Aquarium

R

SEATTLE WATERFRONT PATHWAY

Ferry Terminal

Elliott Bay

N

0   1/2   1
Mile

South Royal Brougham Way

View from Smith Cove Marina.

again under the Magnolia Bridge; a sign directs you to Smith Cove Park across the street and down the sidewalk at mile 3.35 (1.75 miles from Galer Street). Mount Rainier stands white and tall across the water, dwarfing the freighters attached to the pier.

From here, you may want to continue 0.5 mile to the restaurants at Smith Cove Marina. The sidewalk and road end at a narrow strip of grass displaying a spectacular view of the Olympic Mountains across the sound. The marina allows public access until dusk.

The kiosk outside Smith Cove Park highlights some interesting rail and shipping history. The Northern Pacific coal bunker pier was completed here in 1891. Steamers and sailing vessels berthed on either side of this 2,500-foot trestle, loading coal from railroad cars until 1899, when the Great Northern Railway built Piers 88 and 89. This linked the transcontinental railroad to the Orient. In 1912 the Port of Seattle bought the tidal flats that were to become Piers 90 and 91. These 2,530-foot piers, completed in 1921, were the longest earth-filled piers in the world. The U.S. Navy owned them from 1942 to 1976.

When you're ready, turn around and return the way you came.

4   Coal Creek Park Trail

This trek along the Coal Creek Park Trail takes you through a bit of coal-mining history on your way to spectacular Cougar Mountain Park. It offers woodsy tranquility and a great workout close to town.

Activities:

Location: Cougar Mountain, Bellevue, King County

Length: 3 miles

Surface: Dirt and ballast

Wheelchair access: The trail is not wheelchair accessible.

Difficulty: Moderate on the southern end due to bridge crossings, a few hills, and some downed logs. The northern end is easy.

Food: No food is available along the trail.

Rest rooms: There is a portable toilet at the Red Town Trailhead.

Seasons: The trail can be used year-round.

Access and parking: You can park your car and access the trail at either the Coal Creek Parkway Trailhead (the trail's northwestern terminus) or the Red Town Trailhead (its southeastern end). To reach the Coal Creek Trailhead, take exit 10 (Coal Creek Parkway) off I–405 and drive east 1.3 miles to an unmarked pullout on the left. (This pullout is 0.8 mile past the light at Factoria Boulevard Southeast and 0.2 mile past the light at Forrest Drive, at a low point in the road.)

For the Red Town Trailhead, take exit 13 off I–90 and turn south onto Lakemont Boulevard Southeast. Drive 3 miles. Where the road curves sharply right, turn left; the trail begins across the street.

Rentals: There are no rentals along the route.

Contact: King County Parks, (206) 296–4232, www.metrokc.gov/parks/atlas/atlas2/mainfrm.htm.

Bus route: #219. The #219 bus passes the Red Town Trailhead and travels within 1 mile of the Coal Creek Parkway Trailhead. Flag it down for a ride. For more information call Metro Transit at (206) 553–3000; or visit the Web site at transit.metrokc.gov.

* *

Newcastle coal was once the best in the Northwest, and the mining industry reached its heyday here from the late nineteenth century through the early twentieth. Unfortunately, Washington State let ownership of the mines fall into the hands of San Francisco moguls. While they reaped the mining profits, Seattle businessmen made what money they could by moving the coal—via the Seattle Walla Walla Railroad—from the mines to steamers destined for transport to San Francisco and beyond. This railroad, Seattle's own, ran to Renton and to the bunkers at the King Street Pier. Due to the powerful politics of railroading and the interests of the Tacoma-based Northern Pacific, however, it never actually reached Walla Walla.

The Coal Creek Park Trail offers a 3-mile trip through this rich history. Much of the land in this area and in surrounding neighborhoods was mined for coal; it's now riddled with underground, artificial caves. In the mines' heyday, disposal of coal tailings built the ravine walls you'll see above the trail. Due to unstable ground and slides, little of the pathway remains on the railroad grade. But it will take you up and down small hills, beside a creek, and to a waterfall on your way to Cougar Mountain Park. You'll cross a variety of bridges that range from a questionable strip of wood, to an artful log with a single rail of round timber, to what looks like a suburban patio.

The trail can be accessed from either end. This description begins at the northwestern terminus and travels southeast to Cougar Mountain. Leaving the Coal Creek Parkway Trailhead, the trail descends into a man-made ravine as it follows the creek, rising above it and crossing it several times. You'll leap over mossy fallen logs and tree roots on this narrow end of the trail; it can be muddy. Leave the creek to climb to an open plateau at about 1 mile.

The Primrose Trail intersects the trail several times, offering an alternate route. You'll find an intersection of both trails at mile 1.7, and the Cinder Cone 0.2 mile beyond. The Coal Creek Trail is well signed until it meets the railroad right-of-way. Turn right onto the right-of-way, then left after a few yards. Cross a fancy bridge and return to a narrow wooded trail. Trains turned around at the roundhouse here.

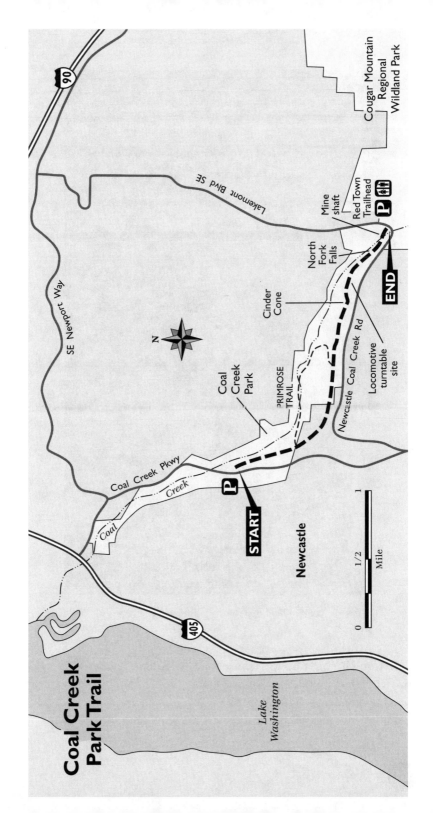

Coal Creek Park Trail

90

Cougar Mountain Regional Wildland Park

Lakemont Blvd SE

Mine shaft

Red Town Trailhead

P

North Fork Falls

SE Newport Way

Cinder Cone

END

N

Coal Creek Park

PRIMROSE TRAIL

Newcastle Coal Creek Rd

Locomotive turntable site

Coal Creek Pkwy

Coal Creek

P

START

Newcastle

405

Lake Washington

0   1/2   1
        Mile

You'll find a wide variety of interesting bridges along the Coal Creek Park Trail.

Before climbing up to Newcastle–Coal Creek Road and the Red Town Trailhead, you'll arrive at a peaceful rest stop. Watch a waterfall slide down a rock face into the creek. Just beyond, cross a bridge to the left to view an old mine. At the trail's end, cross Lakemont

Boulevard Southeast (which becomes Newcastle-Coal Creek Road) to reach the Red Town Trailhead. Here, check the trail map to review a century of coal mining on Cougar Mountain. In 1883 the Red Town Trailhead was a mining town, population 750.

You're now in Cougar Mountain Park, which covers more than 3,000 acres and is the largest of the King County parks. The Issaquah Alps range here predates the Cascade Mountains, possibly dating back 8,000 years. There are 36 miles of hiking trails and more than 12 miles for equestrians. Wetlands and creeks originate within the park, which is forested by western red cedar, western hemlock, Douglas fir, Sitka spruce, and big-leaf maple. Keep your eyes open for black-tailed deer, black bears, bobcats, coyotes, bald eagles, ravens, sharp-shinned hawks, and pileated woodpeckers.

Other Cougar Mountain attractions include coal-mining shafts, spectacular waterfalls, a restored meadow (it was a baseball field in the 1920s), the former townsite, mountaintop views, large glacier boulders, numerous caves, and—surprisingly—a former missile site. After World War II, anti-aircraft guns were placed on Cougar Mountain. During the Cold War, these gunbases were upgraded to Nike missile and radar sites. The park offers interpretive programs to guide you through all of the history and natural resources of the park.

When you're ready, turn around and return the way you came.

This 15-mile trail offers a study in contrasts: from the bustling Supermall with its endless shops to small-town Algona, which looks straight out of the nineteenth century; from the imposing architecture of the Emerald Downs Race Track to the majesty of Mount Rainier; from industry to agriculture, it's all here.

Activities:

Location: King County, from Tukwila to Pacific, and including the towns of Kent, Auburn, and Algona

Length: 15 miles

Surface: Asphalt with soft shoulders

Wheelchair access: Yes, along most of the trail. There are two handicapped parking spots at South 277th Street in Kent, and there's easy access to the trail from the Kent Transit Center at James Street, Kent.

Difficulty: Easy

Food: In the town of Algona, you'll find restaurants, grocery stores, and espresso shops adjacent to the trail. The Supermall in Auburn has multiple restaurants. Downtown Kent (with lots of fast food) is several blocks east of the trail at Smith Street.

Rest rooms: You'll find both rest rooms and drinking water at Kent Uplands Playfield and at General Services Administration (GSA) Park in Auburn (where the rest rooms are located across an active railroad track).

Seasons: The trail can be used year-round.

Access and parking: You can access the trail from several points along the way. At its northern terminus in Tukwila, you can park at Bicentennial Park, located on the west side of the Green River on Strander Boulevard, 1 block west of West Valley Highway. Cross West Valley Highway on Strander to dead-end at the trail. (It extends north for 0.42 mile from here.) Another pathway, the Green River Trail—which is depicted on the map but not described here—also passes through Bicentennial Park. You can head south on this trail and loop north on the Interurban or the reverse. The trails intersect again at Foster Park.

To start at the Foster Park Trailhead, exit Route 167 at Willis Street in Kent. Head east to Central Avenue. Turn right and head south to 259th Street. Turn right (west) and pass under a trestle to reach a parking lot on your left.

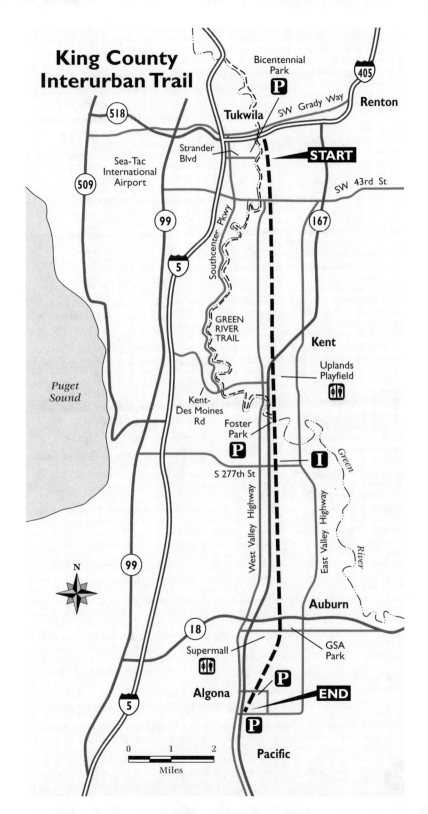

You can also start at either Algona or Pacific, at the southern end of the trail. To park in Algona, exit Route 167 at Algona-Pacific and head east on Ellingson Road. Then turn north onto Milwaukee Boulevard South to park on First Avenue in Algona. To reach the tiny lot at the trail's southern terminus in Pacific, head south on Milwaukee Boulevard, then west on Third Avenue.

Finally, street parking or small dirt lots are available at many intersections along the way.

Rentals: You can rent in-line skates at Play It Again Sports at 17622 108th Street SE in Renton; (425) 227–8777. For bike rental in Puget Sound, see Appendix A.

Contact: King County Parks, (206) 296–4232, www.metrokc.gov/parks/atlas/atlas2/mainfrm.htm or www.metrokc.gov/parks.

Bus routes: Bus #150 runs from Seattle and Tukwila to Auburn. It can be easily reached from the trail in Tukwila; at the Kent Transit Center; 0.8 mile east of the trail on 37th Street Northwest and Auburn Way; and other points south along Auburn Way. For more information call Metro Transit at (206) 553–3000; or visit the Web site at transit.metrokc.gov.

• •

The electric Interurban Railway transported people from Seattle to Tacoma from September 1902 until December 1928. It ran first as the Interurban Railway, then the Seattle Electric Company, and finally the Puget Sound Electric Railway. At sixty cents one way (a dollar round trip), this was a highly successful run until automobiles arrived in the 1920s. The transportation of goods from the productive soil of the Green River Valley to local markets accounted for 20 percent of the load.

Farming and manufacturing still dominate this route. Large warehouses, office parks, highways, malls, and hotels will follow you south from Tukwila to Pacific on the King County Interurban Trail. Pastureland, rivers, and parks parallel the trail as well. People magnets like the Supermall, Emerald Downs Race Track, and Boeing back up against your pathway. The location of the trail near industry, highways, and buses allows commuters to travel via a combination of trails, buses, and cars. It also provides miles of parkland for residents of industrial neighborhoods.

Although the trail can be accessed from many points along the way, this description carries you from its northern end, in Tukwila,

The Big Brother and Little Brother trestles of the King County Interurban Trail can be seen from the Green River Trail at Foster Park.

south to Pacific. Depart from Strander Boulevard in Tukwila heading south. You'll travel between active railroad and office parks, under power lines, and through open fields.

At mile 5 pass under Route 167 and continue to the playing fields and the skate park at Smith Street in downtown Kent. To cross Willis Street at mile 6, you'll jog right to cross at the light, then jog back left, crossing 74th Avenue South, to regain the trail.

Arrive at Foster Park at 6.5 miles. The park lies at the base of a teal-colored trestle. Pause for a view of the Green River below and notice an active railroad trestle beside you. Look closely: The trail bridge was built in the image of its big brother. (Indeed, it's called the Little Brother.) Two active tracks straddle the trail to the south. Some carry new cars, some open boxcars. Down the track, a yellow caboose rests still and alone. You're standing in an outdoor museum amid the steel rails of the Union Pacific, the Burlington Northern, and the old path of the Interurban.

The portions of the trail that pass under power lines are supported cooperatively by Puget Sound Energy and the cities along the trail. At South 277th Street, mile 8, approach a kiosk and cross a bridge over the wetlands. Horseback riding is allowed from this point southward on an unmaintained shoulder. Mount Rainier fills the sky here, as it does along most of your route.

At mile 9.5, you are dwarfed by a bright blue-and-green building crawling with contrasting shapes. The Emerald Downs Race Track looms like the Emerald City Palace, high above the gray and brown structures along the pathway. (Some folks take this trail to the races and avoid the traffic!) Check out the kiosk beside the trail as you examine the interesting architecture.

After you cross under several highways, you're suddenly hit by orange neon signs. This is the popular Supermall (check out all the tour buses!). Shop, eat, rest—it's all here. If you can't resist the stores here, you'll be happy to know you can hop a bus back to your car. Otherwise, cross the four lanes of 15th Street Southwest at the light as you continue on the trail.

Once you push on past the mall, every sense of urban life disappears. All at once at mile 14, you enter a picture from the past—a grassy little park with a gazebo, people meandering in the small street ahead, kids riding back and forth on their bikes, a restaurant in a timeworn wooden building, and, to your left, an espresso shop along with the local grocery. This is Algona. (Locals tell me, by the way, that there's a second espresso shop down the road; only in

A railroad crossing for trail users in Kent.

The friendly neighborhood of Algona is a welcome change of pace from the urban bustle that surrounds it.

rural Washington do 2,000 residents require two such places!) This little town isn't far from the city of Auburn—just a few blocks. But it seems disconnected from the rest of the world. The residents are friendly and proud to share their history. They'll tell you about the railroad or about their own favorite spots along the trail. The nearby town of Pacific is 1 mile down the trail, but you'll recognize it only by the trail end. Between the two towns you'll cross several roads, most small with little traffic. Utility trucks may be on the trail now and then.

When you're ready, turn around and return the way you came.

Future Plans

The King County Interurban Trail will eventually reach Fort Dent to the north; in the south, it'll extend a few blocks farther in the town of Pacific. The Green River Trail, partly on roads and partly on a trail, makes a nice loop. It will ultimately extend to Alki Point on the Duwamish Trail, offering a great river-to-sound, suburb-to-city tour.

This excursion takes you down a historic corridor in and out of view of busy I-5, whose sea of red taillights competes in autumn with the orange-gold of maple trees, a forest of deeply colored evergreens, and tangles of blackberry bushes.

Activities:

Location: The cities of Everett, Lynnwood, and Mountlake Terrace, all in Snohomish County

Length: 14 miles

Surface: Asphalt

Wheelchair access: Most of the trail is wheelchair accessible.

Difficulty: Easy. The trail is mostly flat, with several hills and several areas that run on the roadside shoulders.

Food: You'll find things to eat in the Alderwood Mall, and at the northern trailhead at Beverly Boulevard; there are roadside eateries along the way, too.

Rest rooms: Rest rooms and drinking water can be found in commercial establishments along the way and in the parks.

Seasons: The trail can be used year-round. Some sections may be closed while the Public Utility District (PUD) works on power lines.

Access and parking: There are numerous access points beside the trail. To reach the South Lynnwood Neighborhood Park near the trail's southern end, leave I-5 at exit 179 and drive west on Southwest 220th Street. Turn north onto 66th Avenue West, east onto Southwest 212th Street, north onto 63rd Avenue West, east onto 211th Street, and north onto 61st Avenue. Leave your car beside the park.

The southern terminus of the trail is about 1.25 miles south of the park in Mountlake Terrace. There is limited parking along this southern end of the trail. If you are commuting from the southern end, you can park on the residential streets that cross the trail or you can park at Ballinger Park next to Lake Ballinger at 228th Street/Lakeview Drive. From Ballinger Park you can walk or ride along 74th Avenue north to the trailhead at 226th Street.

To begin toward the northern end of the trail, leave I-5 at exit 189 and follow Route 526 westbound toward Evergreen Way. Turn right onto Campus Parkway, then right onto Casino Road to park at Cascade High School in Everett. The trail begins across Casino Road.

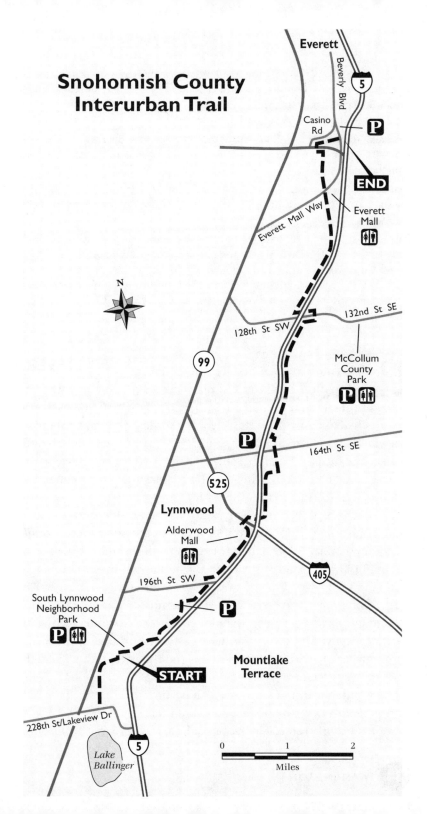

Snohomish County
Interurban Trail

Everett

Beverly Blvd

I-5

P

Casino
Rd

END

Everett Mall Way

Everett
Mall

N

128th St SW

132nd St SE

99

McCollum
County
Park
P

P

164th St SE

525

Lynnwood

Alderwood
Mall

I-405

196th St SW

South Lynnwood
Neighborhood
Park
P

P

START

**Mountlake
Terrace**

228th St/Lakeview Dr

I-5

*Lake
Ballinger*

0   1   2

Miles

You can also park along the residential streets in Mountlake Terrace; at the Alderwood Mall Boulevard Park & Ride (46th Avenue West and 202nd Street Southwest); at the McCollum County Park (600 128th Street Southwest); or at the 164th Street Park & Ride.

Rentals: You can rent in-line skates from Play It Again Sports at 19513 Highway 99 in Lynnwood; (425) 670–1184. For bike rentals in Puget Sound, see Appendix A.

Contacts: Snohomish County Parks, (425) 388–6600, www.co.snohomish.wa.us/parks/intrubnp.htm; Snohomish County Visitors Bureau, (425) 348–5802

Bus routes: Use bus #610 along Route 99. Board the bus at Route 99 and Cascade High School; at Everett near the northern trailhead, Route 99, and 208th Street Southwest; or at Lynnwood near the South Lynnwood Neighborhood Park. For more information check out the Community Transit Web site at www.commtrans.org. You can also call them at (800) 562–1375 or (425) 353–RIDE.

. . . .

P eople came to town first by canoe, then riverboat, and finally train. With the rail lines in place across the Northwest, trains and mosquito fleets shuttled the settlers from town to town, but passengers had to compete with freight schedules, and most inland areas were without service. Then, on April 30, 1910, the Everett-Seattle Interurban introduced an elegant and effective way to move people between neighborhoods. This—the longest-lasting interurban line in Washington—connected Seattle with Everett for twenty-nine years, over a distance of 29 miles. The trolley carried residents to the Playland Amusement Park at Bitter Lake and to the Snohomish County Fairgrounds near Silver Lake; it hauled soldiers and it transported paving bricks for the construction of the Bothell-Everett Highway. In the end, however, it could not compete with cars and buses. "The line, which once traversed beautiful stands of virgin timber and skirted limpid lakes, will be abandoned and the customers along the right of way will be served by sleek gasoline-burning buses, whose coming years ago foretold the doom of the Interurban cars," said the *Everett Daily Herald* in 1939.

Now a public utilities corridor, the portion of this trail that reaches from South Lynnwood north to Everett lets you overtake I–5 gridlock on a historic route. The maple trees and blackberry bushes help distract you from the traffic, and as you approach the northern trailhead, the trail moves away from the highways. The quiet small-town ambience will greet and soothe you.

You can access the Snohomish County Interurban Trail from many points along the way; this description will guide you from South Lynnwood Neighborhood Park at its southern end northward. As you depart the park the Interurban logo guides you through the park, onto the roadside, and finally between Alderwood Mall and I–5. At Alderwood Mall Boulevard (also 26th Avenue West) at South Maple Road, a trail sign points right. Go uphill on South Maple Road for 0.5 mile. Beware the occasional glass, gravel, and dirt on the shoulder. Cross the freeway bridge and take the next right, Butternut Road. Turn right onto the trail. Now on the east side of I 5, you pass a sea of red taillights. In autumn the orange-gold of maple trees highlights the forest of deeply colored evergreens and blackberries. The trail is well marked in most places.

You'll next head uphill, curving sharply east just south of 164th Street, at mile 4.5. Turn left (north) where the trail reaches a T-intersection at 13th Street, which becomes Meadowbrook (this left turn is unmarked). Pass through a light on 13th, then turn left at 160th Street Southwest at 5 miles. The trail sign is on your left, just after you start downhill. Use caution crossing the road. As you return to the I–5 corridor, blue spruce, tall firs, and banks of blackberry bushes shield you from the highway.

At exit 186 (Paine Field; mile 7.5) the trail escapes I–5 and passes by an old drive-in, now the Puget Park Swap Meet and Drive-In. Turn left at Third Avenue Southwest where the trail becomes a sidewalk. At mile 7.75, turn left on 128th Street (a stoplight) to find espresso, granita, and snacks at Sydney's Coffee Company.

Cross I–5 on 128th Street Southwest. Use caution on the ramp. You'll regain the trail on the west side of the interstate after crossing the off ramp. The light there makes this a safer crossing.

Now a high cement wall separates you from the freeway. The tall cedars and firs all but block the traffic noise.

The trail continues straight as a sidewalk at West Mall Drive and crosses Southeast Everett Mall Way. Turn left at 89th Street Southwest (mile 11.5), then right at Seventh Avenue Southeast (a stoplight) and right at East Casino Road (another stoplight). Pass under the highway.

The trail takes a right across from Cascade High School. Enjoy the calm of a residential neighborhood and some picnic tables. Head downhill into the Pinehurst neighborhood and cross Beverly Street. You'll discover a restaurant or two and the neighborhood convenience store in a nifty old building. Use the crosswalk here—not only for safety, but also to enjoy the unusual signal: It flashes a bicycle symbol just like the ones found in downtown Zurich. Pass through the Beverly Park substation to the trail's end at Interurban Park on Madison (mile 13.5). Stop to rest in the park or cross the street to the Treasure Shack, a rural antiques store. When you're ready, turn around and return the way you came.

Future Plans

The city of Mountlake Terrace will ultimately extend the trail south to the King County line. Edmonds is contemplating alternative alignments for the corridor; an overpass over I–5 north of 128th Street has been proposed as a way to avoid the interchange. Everett plans to extend the trail to the downtown neighborhood. Portions of the corridor are reserved for a passenger rail line.

7 Cedar River Trail and Lake Wilderness Trail

Beginning as a narrow path below the streets of Renton, the Cedar River Trail ascends to street level to head east toward Maple Valley and Landsburg Park. The final miles of rural, wooded pathway visit the Cedar River at its most dramatic. A side trip to Lake Wilderness offers the chance for a waterfront picnic.

Activities:

Location: The cities of Renton and Maple Valley, along with Lake Wilderness, all in King County

Length: The Cedar River Trail runs 17.5 miles; the Lake Wilderness Trail is a 4-mile trip.

Surface: Asphalt, ballast (some of it heavy), and dirt

Wheelchair access: There are paved portions of trail at Riverview Park, Liberty Park, North Sixth Street, Wells Street, and Cedar River Park.

Difficulty: Mostly easy, although several miles between Cedar Grove Road and the Route 18 overpass are difficult due to large, deep ballast.

Food: Grocery stores and restaurants can be found in Renton, Lake Wilderness, and Maple Valley.

Rest rooms: Most of the park facilities listed under "Access and parking" have vault toilets or rest rooms, along with drinking water, phones, picnic tables, barbecues, and picnic shelters. Check the Web sites listed under "Contact" for more facilities.

Seasons: The trail can be used year-round.

Access and parking: You can park your car and access the trail at any of the following park facilities:

- *North Sixth Street at the Cedar River:* If you're coming from I–405 South, take exit 5 (Park Avenue/Sunset Boulevard Northeast). Turn right from the exit onto Park Avenue, then turn right onto North Sixth Street. Continue straight for several blocks until you dead-end at the trail. You'll pass a large trail sign at Logan Street. The road turns right to parallel the trail. You can park at the edge of Puget Sound. This is the western terminus of the Cedar River Trail.

  If you're arriving from I–405 North, take exit 5 (Issaquah/Sunset Boulevard Northeast). Turn left onto Sunset Boulevard, which will eventually turn into Park Avenue. Turn right onto North Sixth Street and continue as directed above.

- *Cedar River and Riverview Parks on Route 169:* From I–405 South, take exit 4 (Maple Valley). This will bring you onto Sunset Boulevard Northeast. Turn left at the second traffic light onto Maple Valley Road (Route 169). Get into the right lane, travel a short distance, and turn right into Cedar River Park. Riverview Park is 1 mile farther, on your right, down a lightly wooded, paved trail. Read about salmon habitat in this little roadside facility.

    From I–405 North, take exit 4A (Renton/Maple Valley). Turn right at the end of the exit onto Maple Valley Road (Route 169), then continue as directed above.

- *Maple Valley Trailhead:* The Maple Valley Trail begins at an unmarked pull-out on Route 169 just west of the Route 18 overpass.

- *Landsburg Park:* Leave I–90 at exit 17 and drive south on Front Street, which turns into 276th Avenue Southeast. Pass through the town of Hobart and south of Southeast 216th Street, 13 miles in all, to the river. Watch for the hang gliders on Tiger Mountain and enjoy the Bavarian setting of Boehms Chocolates in Issaquah along the way. Park in the lot on 276th Avenue Southeast across from Landsburg Park. This is the eastern terminus of the Cedar River Trail.

    You can also drive east on 216th Street from Route 169 in Maple Valley to its end at 276th Avenue. Turn right to reach the river in 2.5 miles.

- *Lake Wilderness Park in Maple Valley:* From Route 169, turn south onto Witte Road Southeast, then left onto Southeast 248th Street after 0.8 mile. The park is on your left in 0.5 mile. The trail begins at the Wilderness Center Lodge; it's 1.8 miles to the Cedar River Trail.

Rentals: You can rent in-line skates at Play It Again Sports, 17622 108th Avenue SE in Renton; (425) 227–8777. See Appendix A for bike rental in Puget Sound. Boat rentals are available at Lake Wilderness.

Contact: King County Parks, (206) 296–4232, www.metrokc.gov/parks/atlas/atlas2/mainfrm.htm or www.metrokc.gov/parks/trails/trails/cedar.htm; or contact City of Renton Parks, (425) 430–6600, www.ci.renton.wa.us

Bus routes: Buses #143 and #149 take you from Seattle to Renton and Maple Valley. The bus depot is at Third and Burnett in Renton; there's a parking lot at Fourth and Burnett. For more information visit the Metro Transit Web site at transit.metrokc.gov, or call them at (206) 553–3000.

•   •   •   •   •   •   •   •   •   •   •   •   •   •   •   •   •   •   •   •

From 1884 to the 1940s, the rail lines you'll be traveling on this jaunt served the coal industry, which was largely responsible for the area's economic growth. The Columbia & Puget Sound Rail-

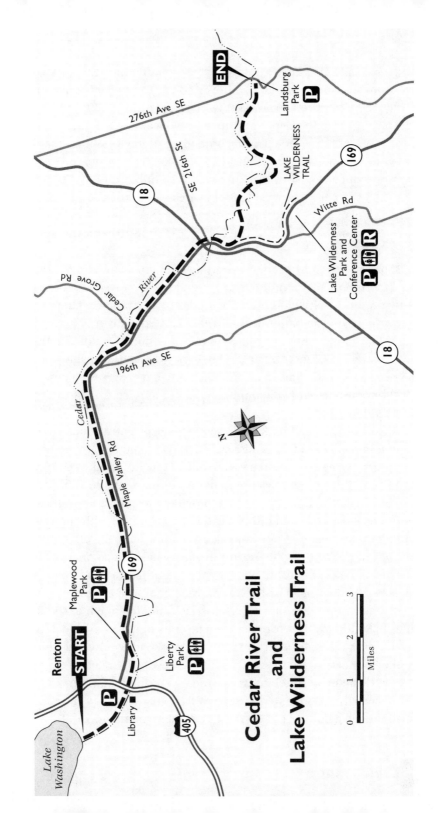

Cedar River Trail
and
Lake Wilderness Trail

way, once called the Seattle Coal & Transportation Company, moved coal from the mines of Maple Valley and Renton to Seattle starting in 1884. One hundred coal cars traveled this route in 1891; by 1913, 236 were making the trip. The Chicago, Milwaukee & Puget Sound Railway, part of the same parent company, ran the lines from Maple Valley to Cedar Falls and Rattlesnake Lake. The mines in Puget Sound produced most of Washington's 1.25 million tons of coal in 1890, and the best coal was from this area—in particular, the Newcastle mine on this line just north of Renton. (See Trail 4, Coal Creek Park.) The coal was taken to the coal docks in Seattle for transport to San Francisco.

You can access the set of trails discussed here from many points; this description begins at the western end, in Renton, and proceeds eastward. In the city of Renton, the Cedar River Trail originates as a narrow path on the banks of the canal-like Cedar River; the city library floats above the water like a modern Ponte Vecchio. The trail then ascends to street level at Liberty Park to head east beside Route 169 on paved trail. This is a safe alternative to a narrow highway, great for commuters, and complete with bus service from Seattle to Maple Valley.

Dressed with treed parks, this section is especially popular with skaters; horseback riding is allowed once you're outside the Renton city limits. It's hard to believe you're only a few hundred yards from Route 169. The trail follows the Cedar River along Route 169, dropping below the highway at times to provide a respite from traffic. It continues close to the highway for the next 5 miles, with the river coming up to meet you now and again, then wandering off, only to return under an old trestle or running along beside you once again.

The paved trail ends at 196th Avenue Southeast (also known as Jones Road); it turns to ballast 1.5 miles farther east at Cedar Grove Road. This surface sucks you in like quicksand for much of the 2.5 miles to Southeast 216th Street. Even fat tires fight to stay afloat. An alternative to this difficult surface is Byres Road Southeast, which parallels the trail from Cedar Grove Road east for 1 mile.

Pass through a tunnel under Southeast 216th Street, then cross a trestle over the Cedar River. Retreat from the highway here and travel though a quiet, rural corridor near the river and its rural river-

The Cedar River Trail follows the scenic Cedar River.

front homes all the way to Landsburg Park. You'll reach the Lake Wilderness cutoff 0.8 mile from the Route 18 overpass (the high overpass above the trailhead pullout). You can take a soft right uphill on the 1.8-mile trail here to reach Lake Wilderness on the Lake Wilderness Trail if you like; see "Alternative Trail," below.

This description, however, continues straight 4.8 miles to Landsburg Park. Along the final 2 miles of this pathway, the Cedar River leaves the trail then sneaks back, crossing back and forth, sometimes wandering with you for a while. Stop on the trestle to watch the river rush, especially when the waters are high. Watch the kayakers fighting the white water. The turbulence and speed of the Cedar River is impressive and frightening during high waters and flood stage. The surrounding terrain is hillier here, near the Cascade Mountains. In Landsburg Park itself you can walk beside the dam. When you're ready, turn around and return the way you came.

Alternative Trail

To enjoy the rural portion of this outing by foot, horse, or mountain bike, try a trip between Lake Wilderness Park and Landsburg Park. Both parks offer pretty waterfront places to picnic, and Lake Wilderness is the site of a large 1890s resort. The early 1900s brought a homestead for fishermen and hunters, which then gave way to the resorts of the 1920s. Some 9,000 guests per day could enjoy the skating rink, dance pavilions, beach slides, trapezes, and diving towers at Gaffney's Grove Resort in 1939. Peek in at the award-winning Lake Wilderness Center to see the modern replacement.

To reach the Cedar River Trail from the lodge, turn left once you reach the wide trail. A gate points you toward the Cedar River Trail, 1.8 miles ahead. The trail surface is easy to ride on a bike or a horse and pleasant to walk. This is an equestrian area. Be kind to the horses. Pass through the forest and the South King County Arboretum with its wandering interpretive trails, under Witte Road Southeast, and beside a housing development. At mile 1.5 you can take a right to enjoy some lovely water views. Trees frame the view of Lake Wilderness from the north bank. It's a great spot for a stroll or a mostly flat ride. Then return to the trail, pass under Route 169, and intersect the Cedar River Trail; Landsburg Park is 4.8 miles to your right.

Future Plans

The trail will be paved an additional 5 miles toward Maple Valley in 2001. Farther in the future is a connection from Landsburg Park to the Snoqualmie Valley Trail (see Trail 10) and the John Wayne Pioneer Trail (see Trail 25) at Rattlesnake Lake in North Bend. Though the railroad right-of-way through the watershed is preserved for trail use, it will only be passable when Seattle shifts to a filtration system.

Tiger Mountain State Forest has several trailheads and miles of trails. Three multiuse rail-trails and one hiking trail follow old railroad grades. The Preston Railroad Trail, the Northwest Timber Trail, and the Iverson Trail can be traveled individually or as a continuous loop. The Preston Railroad and Northwest Timber Trails take you on an exhilarating up- and downhill ride; the Iverson Trail, which makes a nice side trip, takes you through lowlands. Mountain bikers maintain these trails and use them heavily, though hikers and equestrians are welcome.

Activities:

Location: King County

Length: 8 miles

Surface: Crushed stone, rocks, gravel, and dirt. You'll find tree roots, puddles, and (on the Preston Railroad Trail section) running water on the pathway.

Wheelchair access: The trail is not wheelchair accessible.

Difficulty: Difficult to expert

Food: No food is available along this trail.

Rest rooms: You'll find facilities on West Side Road, at the Iverson Trailhead parking lot.

Seasons: Tiger Mountain State Forest trails are open from April 16 through October 14.

Access and parking: To reach the Tiger Summit Parking Lot, get off I–90 at exit 25 (Route 18). Head west 4.3 miles to the TIGER MOUNTAIN SUMMIT sign. The lot is just beyond on the right.

You can also access the Iverson Railroad Trail from a second parking lot. To reach this from the main lot, drive through the left-hand gate onto West Side Road. A locked gate marks the parking, rest rooms, and trailhead.

Rentals: See Appendix A for bike rentals in Puget Sound.

Contact: Washington State Department of Natural Resources, (800) 527–3305

Bus routes: None

* * * * * * * * * * * * * * * * * * * *

L ogging in Tiger Mountain State Forest started in the 1920s and continues today. Timber was transported by switchback or incline railways to the base of the mountain and by local railroads to mills in Preston, Issaquah, Hobart, and High Point. Both the Preston and Northwest Timber Trails were originally switchback railways. Where the trail now turns sharply at each switchback, a tail track once extended straight ahead to allow trains to move past the switchback, then back up to continue downhill. The Iverson Trail was part of the Wooden Pacific incline railway, which climbed 2 straight miles to the summit. The trails are named for the companies that logged them. The last of them, the Preston Mill, burned down twelve years ago. The Department of Natural Resources, together with mountain bikers, built the trails in the early 1990s. The West Tiger Railroad Grade, a hiking trail, starts at the inner reaches of the West Tiger Natural Resources Conservation Area and is reached from the High School Trail (see "More Washington Rail-Trails" for information).

While you're on the road, watch out for logging trucks and communications vehicles for the radio, television, and cell-phone towers. Gates are locked year-round, blocking other traffic. The trails are closed during the wet season, because costly damage can occur when they're muddy.

There are many trails and routes to take as you explore Tiger Mountain. This description takes you up the Preston Railroad Trail, whose summit (at 1,230 feet) lies 3.4 miles above the parking lot via Main Tiger Mountain Road. Once you complete the Preston segment, you'll descend the Northwest Timber Trail back to the parking lot or (if you'd like to stretch your legs some more) to the Connector Trail, which leads to the Iverson Railroad Trail.

Preston Railroad Trail, 3.7 miles

Tough, wet, and fun: That's the expert-level Preston Railroad Trail. You've got to like to biff and bounce on a bike, wade through puddles, straddle streams, and rocket off roots. A single-track downhill grade that turns into a series of switchbacks, the trail is currently a drainage, though culverts are being added to dry it out. The Backcountry Bicycle Trail Club has adopted the trail; we have its members to thank for maintenance.

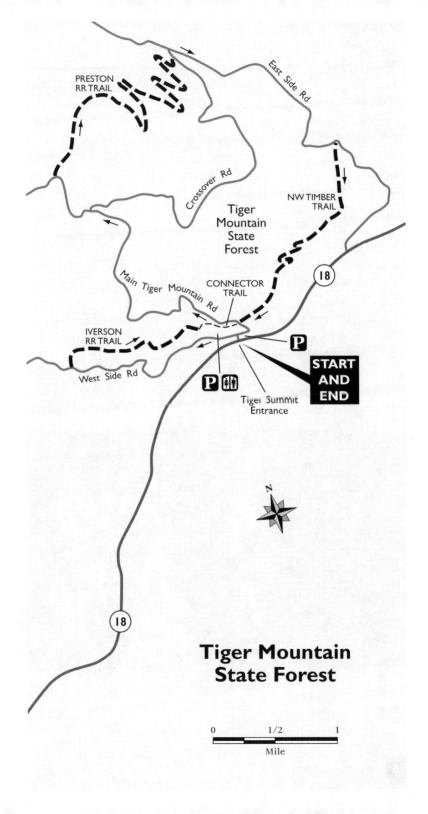

PRESTON
RR TRAIL

East Side Rd

Crossover Rd

Tiger
Mountain
State
Forest

NW TIMBER
TRAIL

18

Main Tiger Mountain Rd

CONNECTOR
TRAIL

IVERSON
RR TRAIL

P

START
AND
END

P

West Side Rd

Tiger Summit
Entrance

N

18

**Tiger Mountain
State Forest**

0   1/2   1
Mile

From the Tiger Mountain Summit parking lot, pass through the right-hand gate. On your way up Main Tiger Mountain Road, you'll pass both the lower trailhead for the Northwest Timber Trail and the Connector Trail that leads to the Iverson Trail. Prepare for a steep climb. The clear-cuts are ugly but allow far-reaching views of Mount Rainier and the Green, Cedar, and White River Valleys. You'll find mile markers on the road and along the trail. At the T-intersection, turn left. The trailhead is a wooden gate on your right. The trail heads briefly and gradually uphill before it begins the long descent. It's narrow, a bit curvy, and fun for an experienced biker. At 0.7 mile, it finds the railroad right-of-way. The roots and obstacles thicken. You're in a forest of fir, cedar, hemlock, alder, and maple trees with bears, bobcats, grouse, ducks, and more than a hundred species of birds.

At approximately 1 mile, look for the first switchback—a hard left. The trail appears to continue straight here. If you miss the switchback, you'll end up at a major drainage; turn back. The trees at switchbacks are often marked with flagging and brush. The switchbacks are quite obvious from here on. Enjoy the challenge of this bumpy, wet descent.

The moist and wooded trails of Tiger Mountain.

Congratulate yourself when you reach the wooden gate at the bottom of the trail. Turn left onto Crossover Road, then right 0.2 mile later onto East Side Road, toward the Northwest Timber Trail. Roads and trails are well signed. Take rocky East Side Road about 2 miles. Relax. Enjoy the rushing water at creek crossings and the valley views. At just under 2 miles, the Northwest Timber Trail departs on your right for some rolling single-track. (East Side Road continues straight to end at Route 18 more than a mile west of the parking lot. Don't continue downhill on this road unless you enjoy a highway stroll!)

Northwest Timber Trail, 2.3 miles

The Northwest Timber trail runs deep in the forest. Small bridges cross drainages and large bridges cross creeks as the pathway winds around the edge of the hillside. The lower end of the trail passes through archways canopied by brightly mossed deciduous trees; the spot captures the colors and essence of a Grimm Brothers fairy-tale painting. Lots of large puddles straddle the trail—prepare for wet feet—which is rugged in places but definitely an octave down from the Preston Railroad Trail in grade, surface, wetness, and obstacles. Check out the open views of the valleys below. Remember: Bikes yield to hikers yield to horses (though this is really bike territory). Use caution on your descents.

At the end of the Northwest Timber Trail, you have two choices. You can either turn left to reach the main parking lot and the end of your outing, or you can cross Main Tiger Mountain Road and find the Connector Trail just uphill. Take this to the Iverson Trail and more exercise.

By the way, you can also travel just the Northwest Timber Trail in an out-and-back trip. From the parking lot, head 0.25 mile up Main Tiger Mountain Road (right-hand gate), then turn right onto the Northwest Timber Trail. You'll ascend to East Side Road, 30 feet higher. Don't let this deceive you: You'll have plenty of little ups and downs on the way. From the road, turn around and return the way you came.

Iverson Railroad Trail, 2 miles

Get ready for a single-track with a long climb and a sometimes difficult descent. Bounce over roots, ride through streams, cross over bridges, and struggle to stay on switchbacks. Cyclists, prepare to walk.

You can explore the Iverson Railroad Trail on its own, or as a continuation of your Northwest Timber Trail jaunt. Start from the main parking lot and pass through the left gate (it is signed). After a bit of an uphill grade, pass through the locked gate onto West Side Road, and continue for 1.5 miles to the signed Iverson Railroad Trail, on your right. Climb through the forest for just under 1.5 miles. The climb is steepest in the first 0.5 mile. Light filters through the dark forest at the top of the trail. Start your descent at a bridge crossing. Prepare to hop or dismount at the treacherous tree trunks and timber across the trail. You'll parallel the West Side Road as you descend the final portion of the trail. Turn right at the T-intersection to return to the trailhead or head left to continue onto the Connector Trail.

9 Preston-Snoqualmie Trail

This peaceful, wooded trail in the Cascade foothills ends with a view of spectacular Snoqualmie Falls. For a romantic walk, an evening ride, your daily jog, or a pleasant skate, this trail is the ticket.

Activities:

Location: Preston, King County

Length: 6.2 miles

Surface: Asphalt with brief, steep gravel switchbacks

Wheelchair access: The trail is wheelchair accessible except for the descent and switchbacks listed below.

Difficulty: Easy, except for a steep paved descent to a road crossing and gravel switchbacks back up to the trail.

Food: In Preston you'll find a mini mart and restaurant at the I–90 interchange. There are restaurants and grocery stores in Fall City. And look for Greenbank Farms cheese and gourmet store west of the trailhead on Preston–Fall City Road.

Rest rooms: There is a chemical toilet at the Lake Alice Road Trailhead.

Seasons: The trail can be used year-round.

Access and parking: You can access the trail from either the Preston or the Lake Alice Road Trailhead. To reach the Preston Trailhead, near the trail's western terminus, leave I–90 at exit 22 (Fall City). Turn north and drive to the T-intersection with Preston–Fall City Road. Turn right (east), drive 2 blocks, and then turn left onto Southeast 87th Place. The small parking lot is on your right.

To avoid the trail's switchbacks and get the grand view, start at the Lake Alice Trailhead (near its eastern end). To reach this trailhead, follow Preston–Fall City Road northeast for 3.5 miles past 87th Street (the location of the Preston Trailhead), then turn right onto Lake Alice Road. You'll find the trailhead on your right in 0.8 mile.

Rentals: There are no rentals along the route. See Appendix A for rentals in Puget Sound.

Contact: King County Department of Open Space, (206) 296–7800, www. metrokc.gov/parks/atlas/atlas2/mainfrm.htm
Bus routes: None

• •

Only a twenty-minute drive from the suburbs on the east side of Lake Washington, the Preston-Snoqualmie Trail makes for a pleasant, woodsy outing. Parents stroll the pathway with their children as locals walk their dogs, enjoying the valley views. The trail ends with a view of Snoqualmie Falls, which drop 270 feet into the Snoqualmie River—100 feet more than the drop at Niagara Falls. The pavement is smooth and relatively flat except for a road crossing with a steep hill on both sides, one paved and the other featuring gravel switchbacks. This Seattle, Lakeshore & Eastern railway was built in 1890; the trail opened in 1978.

This description follows the trail from west to east. The trail actually extends 0.9 mile farther west from its western trailhead in Preston. If you'd like to explore this section, leave the trailhead parking lot and cross Southeast 87th Street; your route parallels the road and winds along the path of a corporate complex. You'll find a few small street crossings, a bit of grade, and some rough pavement here and there—just enough to intimidate a beginning skater.

To head east toward Snoqualmie Falls, start at the edge of the parking lot. The trail traverses a sidehill. The hillside down to the streets of the Preston Mill town and the valley below affords fine views and brightens your jaunt. You may see deer and stellar jays, cougars and bears. Locals mostly ignore the presence of cougars and bears. Though the animals retreat when humans are around, please do read the wildlife guidelines at the trailhead.

A large trestle once crossed the Raging River Valley 2.5 miles out. It has been replaced with a steep descent to the road. Watch for traffic veering around the curve as you cross Preston–Fall City Road. The trail parallels the road briefly, turns left, and climbs back up several steep gravel switchbacks to the hillside. Arrive at the Lake Alice Trailhead 3.5 miles from Preston.

The final 1.8 miles of trail south from Lake Alice Road offer valley views and a distant view of Snoqualmie Falls, framed by tall fir

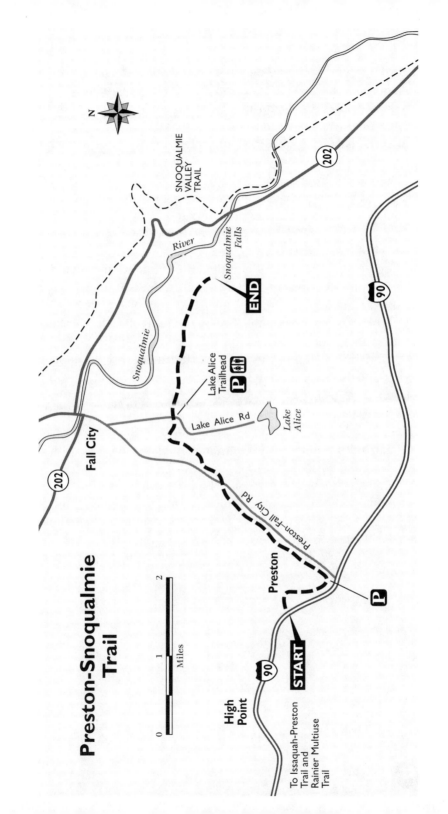

Preston-Snoqualmie Trail

N

0   1   2
Miles

SNOQUALMIE VALLEY TRAIL

202

Snoqualmie River

Snoqualmie Falls

END

Lake Alice Trailhead
P

Lake Alice Rd

Lake Alice

Fall City

202

Preston

Preston-Fall City Rd

90

P

START

90

High Point

To Issaquah-Preston Trail and Rainier Multiuse Trail

and cedar trees. Far from the tourist experience at the Salish Lodge, you'll observe the scene from a secluded bench in the forest.

Visit the nearby town of Fall City for a meal—perhaps beside the Snoqualmie River—or head up to the Salish Lodge for a bird's-eye view of the falls from the attic lounge. Or you can head west from the Preston Trailhead on Preston–Fall City Road to explore Greenbank Farms cheese and gourmet shop, open seven days a week. The folks here will happily pack you a lunch to go.

When you're ready, turn around and return the way you came.

Future Plans

The Snoqualmie Valley Trail and the Snoqualmie Centennial Trail are across the river from the Preston-Snoqualmie Trail. Currently, the Snoqualmie River is uncrossable. The right-of-way beyond the end of the Preston-Snoqualmie Trail is presently used by the Puget Sound Railroad Historical Society. Sight-seeing trains run from the old Snoqualmie depot of the Great Northern Railway to the ledge above the falls. Perhaps in the future this right-of-way ledge can be shared in a way that would allow the Preston-Snoqualmie Trail to cross the river and connect to the other trails of the Snoqualmie Valley, along with the town of Snoqualmie. For now, the train ride from the depot—also a railroad museum—makes for an enjoyable, historic look above the falls.

Eventually the Issaquah-Preston Trail will connect to the Preston-Snoqualmie Trail, the Rainier Multiuse Trail in Issaquah, and the planned Lake Sammamish Trail (see More Washington Rail-Trails). These will all be linked when a new highway interchange is built.

Snoqualmie Valley Trail and Snoqualmie Valley Trail Extension

Wander the foothills of rural Snoqualmie Valley from Duvall through Carnation, to Snoqualmie Falls near Snoqualmie, on to North Bend, and finally to the John Wayne Pioneer Trail. You'll travel near the highway, through wetlands, along ridges, above the valley, through a golf course, minutes from Snoqualmie Falls, and into charming and historic downtown areas. Enjoy a teahouse, an elegant lodge, a 268-foot waterfall, bakeries, bridges, rivers, lakes, and one of the largest logging operations in the Northwest.

Activities:

Location: Duvall to North Bend, King County

Length: 33 miles

Surface: Crushed rock and original ballast. Look out for large, deep gravel on the decked trestles.

Wheelchair access: The trail is not wheelchair accessible.

Difficulty: Easy to moderate. The ballast and trestle gravel is a bit heavy in places. The 2.6 percent average grade above the valley floor requires a few climbs. The roadside trail detour from Tokul Road to Mount Si Golf Course also has some climbs.

Food: Restaurants, cafes, and grocery stores are all found within 1 mile of the trail, in Snoqualmie, Duvall, Carnation, Snoqualmie Falls, and North Bend. Mount Si Golf Course is along the trail as well.

Rest rooms: Public rest rooms are available at Duvall Park and at Rattlesnake Lake Recreation Area. There is also drinking water at Rattlesnake Lake.

Seasons: The trail can be used year-round.

Access and parking: To start at the northern end of the trail in Duvall, take Woodinville-Duvall Road east to Route 203, then turn south onto 203. Or you can head north from Carnation on Route 203. Once in Duvall, look for Stevens Street in the center of town. Turn west and stay left of the fence to park in the McCormick Park lot. To start in North Bend, turn north off North Bend Way, onto Ballarat to reach the Park & Ride lot on Northeast 4th Street, near the library.

To start at Nick Loutsis Park in Carnation, take Route 203 to Entwhistle Street and turn east.

If you want to start the trail at Tokul Road, park at the railroad museum on Railroad Avenue, Snoqualmie, and ride the Snoqualmie Centennial Trail (see page 173) to the stoplight to the north. Cross Route 202, cross the bridge, and turn right on Tokul Road to 60th. Turn right onto the single-track trail down to the railroad grade. You can also descend the steps to the trail, found on Tokul Road at the tunnel.

To begin at Rattlesnake Lake, take exit 32 (436th Avenue Northeast) off I–90 eastbound. Turn south and follow the curves of the road for 2.9 miles to park at Rattlesnake Lake. Find the trail directly across the street.

Rentals: There are no rentals along the route. See Appendix A for bike rentals in Puget Sound.

Contact: King County Parks, (206) 296–4232, www.metrokc.gov/parks/atlas/atlas2/mainfrm.htm

Bus route: On weekdays only, take bus #929 from Duvall to North Bend, or #209 from Preston to Fall City to North Bend. Check the Metro Transit Web site at transit.metrokc.gov or call them at (206) 553–3000.

• •

Y ou can choose from among many spots to hop on the Snoqualmie Valley Trail; this description follows it from Duvall (at its northern end) to Rattlesnake Lake in the south. You may wish to travel from Carnation to Duvall for a flat ride; head to Snoqualmie Falls for some hills and ridge views; or depart from North Bend for a lowland ride away from the highway. Start at Rattlesnake Lake for a longer trip with a bit of downhill grade.

Duvall to Carnation, 9 miles

Enjoy the town of Duvall; watch it hanging on to its rural feel despite recent growth. Look for the antiques shops and ice cream parlor. From McCormick Park, head north a few blocks for a peek at an old Chicago, Milwaukee, St. Paul & Pacific Railroad depot.

The trail travels southeast on the west side of Route 203, close to the road yet separated by wetlands and open fields. You'll pass driveway crossings of the working farms and lots of blackberry bushes. Watch for waterfowl and listen for songbirds. Bird hunters sometimes stalk their prey near the trail, but this is not generally a problem. Use caution at a couple of road crossings.

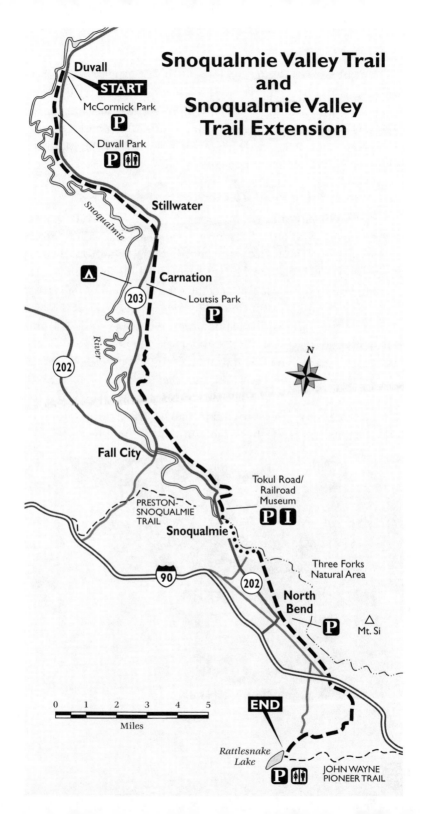

Snoqualmie Valley Trail and Snoqualmie Valley Trail Extension

Duvall

START

McCormick Park

P

Duvall Park

P 🛉🛉

Stillwater

Snoqualmie

🏕️

Carnation

(203)

Loutsis Park

P

River

(202)

N

Fall City

PRESTON-
SNOQUALMIE
TRAIL

Tokul Road/
Railroad
Museum

P **I**

Snoqualmie

Three Forks
Natural Area

(90)

(202)

**North
Bend**

P

△
Mt. Si

| 0 | 1 | 2 | 3 | 4 | 5 |

Miles

END

Rattlesnake
Lake

P 🛉🛉

JOHN WAYNE
PIONEER TRAIL

The trail crosses Route 203 just north of Carnation. Reach the Nick Loutsis Trailhead at mile 9 at Entwhistle Road. Turn west (right) for a neighborhood tour of Carnation, an espresso at Starbucks, a snack at QFC grocery, or tea and fresh muffins at Rosebuds Tea Room and Antique Shop. Take a side trip to the riverfront at Tolt-McDonald Park just south of the shopping center.

Carnation to Tokul Road, 10 miles

From Carnation the trail rises above the Snoqualmie Valley, crossing over trestles and enjoying views of the river and valley through a canopy of evergreens. Cross the Tolt River 0.5 mile from the town of Carnation. You'll pass Remlinger Farms 0.5 mile farther on. Cross the 356th Drive Southeast Trailhead at 7 miles. A high bridge crosses Tokul Creek at 9 miles, affording valley views and a peek at the creek below. The trail climbs near Snoqualmie Falls and ends 3.3 miles from 356th under the Tokul Road underpass at mile 10. Exit the trail via the single-track, heading left up to 60th Street Southeast.

To visit Snoqualmie Falls and take the Snoqualmie Centennial Trail to the Northwest Railroad Museum for a side trip, water, rest rooms, a snack, or a meal, turn left from 60th Street onto Tokul Road. To view the falls, turn right at the T-intersection with Route 202 at

This 1912 depot station in Duvall used to serve the Chicago, Milwaukee, St. Paul & Pacific Railroad.

1.2 miles. Ride the shoulder briefly to the parking lot on your right. Take the bridge to the falls. Do not cross the highway. To reach the museum, turn left after you cross the bridge to the falls for a brief jaunt and a bridge crossing on the road. Leave the road at the light at Snoqualmie Parkway to ride the Snoqualmie Centennial Trail to its end at the museum, 0.8 mile.

Tokul Road to Meadowbrook, 5 miles

To reach the section of trail through North Bend and on to Rattlesnake Lake, turn right onto Tokul Road from 60th Street for a 5-mile rolling ride on a country road. Tokul Road becomes 396th Drive Southeast and then Reinig Road. At 2.3 miles, turn right at the Weyerhauser Mill to see the scope of this eighty-six-year-old logging facility. The mill was the second all-electric mill in the United States and the first to reduce the incidence of forest fires by electrifying the steam donkey logging trains. The mill looms in the midst of rural rolling hills and valleys. It lies on the Snoqualmie River and on the Seattle, Lakeshore & Eastern main line, which hauled timber for shipping. The line reached into Seattle from North Bend and connected to what is now the Snohomish Centennial Trail in Snohomish.

The city of Snoqualmie Falls—the Weyerhauser Company town— dominated the landscape here until 1958. The mill workers' homes were than sold and transported, on a temporary bridge, to the valley below. Beyond the mill, the Snoqualmie River comes into view. The trestle high above your head is the right-of-way you're detouring around. It makes a pretty picture. Don't miss the side trip to the trestle to view Mount Si in the distance from atop the river (see below).

Tokul Road changes names, eventually becoming Reinig Road. Stay left at the Y with Mill Pond Road to pass over Meadowbrook Bridge. Use caution: The bridge is narrow, and traffic curves up onto it at a good clip. You can choose the narrow trail behind the guardrail to ascend onto the wooden bridge walkway. If you do, stop to enjoy the river view. Just a few miles from Snoqualmie Falls, the second most visited tourist attraction in the state, you sit in a town with more past than present, a town with no tourists, little traffic, and several generations of residents. The bridge drops you into the past, the former town of Meadowbrook. Here sit the old Weyerhauser homes. Take a look at the fortlike brick structure that houses local businesses. An iron gate disrupts the redbrick wall, framing a view of Mount Si. Check out the old theater on the corner and photos of Meadowbrook's past in the Harley shop. Originally a huge farm, with the advent of roads and cars it became a town where workers could live independent of Weyerhauser ties.

To continue, turn left at the end of the 1-block town, at Park Street. Find Mount Si Golf Course on your left in 0.7 mile. Take a left into the driveway and a left onto the trail to detour 0.8 mile to the old trestle. If you've got the miles left in your legs, it's worth the sidetrip. Look down across the river and up at Mount Si, towering above and framed by the rust-red railroad bridge. If it's time for lunch, try the deck at the golf course restaurant. It's a friendly place that serves good food. They'll even reserve a table for you and your cycling buddies.

Meadowbrook to North Bend, 2 miles

Head south (right) from the golf course for a short ride with pretty views. Pass through Mount Si Golf Course, beside homes and fields, along the Snoqualmie River, and below the steep wall of Mount Si. Cross several small roads before you reach the parking lot at Fourth and Ballarat. For a bit of railroad history, visit the library across the street; you might also wish to head downtown to visit George's Bakery or the main street of downtown North Bend, just a few minutes away. The factory outlet mall is up the street a couple of miles.

North Bend to Rattlesnake Lake and the John Wayne Pioneer Trail, 7.3 miles

The Snoqualmie Valley Trail Extension continues north of the parking lot. Mount Si remains in sight as you pass soccer fields, cross several streets, and watch the skate rats at the snowboard park. Cross North Bend Way at 2 miles and cross under I–90. Arrive at Rattlesnake Lake 4.75 miles from here. To reach the John Wayne Trail, hop off the trail onto the road and through the gate. Look for the gated trail on your left at 0.6 mile. You can ride east on The John Wayne Trail or enjoy The Rattlesnake Lake Recreation Area.

A stretch of trail from Duvall to Carnation.

Trail Connections and Future Plans

You don't have to cross the country to discover differences, find surprises, and witness dramatic changes in scenery, terrain, culinary treats, and perspective. Existing trails in Washington State combine to create a diverse and scenic experience. For instance, you can travel from Duvall to the Columbia River on the Snoqualmie Valley Trail (SVT) and the John Wayne Pioneer Trail.

You could also spend a day touring Seattle neighborhoods and rural towns, breweries and wineries, espresso shops and bakeries, lakes and rivers, mountains and desert on one continuous trail. The

The Snoqualmie Valley Trail parallels the Snoqualmie River.

SVT will be linked to the Snohomish Centennial Trail through Monroe. The connection between the SVT extension, the John Wayne Trail at Rattlesnake Lake, and the Cedar River Trail will take you to Renton and Lake Washington. If the SVT becomes linked to the Preston-Snoqualmie Trail, you'll continue into Issaquah, up Lake Sammamish to Redmond, and all the way to Seattle for a multiday tour of the Snoqualmie Valley and Seattle. You'll be able to start this tour from the east at the border of Idaho or from the north in Skagit County, once the work is done. Our counties, cities, and the state are working vigorously to develop future trails and connections that will provide an even greater trail network suitable for multiday tours.

This interpretive hiking trail in the Stevens Pass historic district climbs a constant 2.2 percent grade. Kiosks guide you through a trail decorated with wildflowers and forests of ferns, alders, and evergreens. The route offers you views of the Alpine Lakes Wilderness and mountain peaks, rivers and streams, remnants of the railroad, and the 7.8-mile Cascade Tunnel. Mileage markers reflect the original railroad signs, indicating mileage to St. Paul, Minnesota. The trail is named for the logo on the Great Northern trains.

Activities:

Location: King County, near Stevens Pass

Length: 6 miles

Surface: Gravel with concrete binder

Wheelchair access: The 1.2-mile lower grade is barrier-free and wheelchair accessible. Also, 3 miles of barrier-free trail (moderate difficulty) is available from the Wellington Trailhead to the Windy Point Tunnel.

Difficulty: Easy to moderate

Food: No food is available along this trail.

Rest rooms: There are rest rooms at both the Martin Creek and Wellington Trailheads.

Seasons: Winter travel is discouraged due to avalanche risks and snow-covered access.

Access and parking: To reach the Martin Creek Trailhead, take Route 2 to milepost 55, 6 miles east of the town of Skykomish, or to milepost 58.4 at Scenic, 5.6 miles west of the summit. Turn north onto the Old Cascade Highway, U.S. Forest Service Road 67. Proceed to Forest Road 6710 (2.3 miles from milepost 55 or 1.4 miles from milepost 58.4). Take Forest Road 6710 1.4 miles to the trailhead.

To reach the Wellington Trailhead, drive to the Stevens Pass parking lot on the north side of Route 2 (opposite the ski area). Heading west, take the first right (0.3 mile) onto Old Stevens Pass Highway at milepost 64.4. After 2.8 miles, turn right onto a short gravel spur road marked WELLINGTON TRAILHEAD.

You'll need a Northwest Forest Pass to park. You can purchase a one-day

($5) or annual ($30) permit via the Internet, the Skykomish Ranger station, or hiking stores.

Rentals: No rentals are available along this trail.

Contact: U.S. Forest Service, Skykomish, (360) 677–2414, www.bcc.ctc.edu/cpsha/irongoat. For an interpretive hikes schedule, group scheduling, or to order the trail guidebook, call (206) 283–1440.

You can also visit the Mount Baker-Snoqualmie Forest Service Web site at www.fs.fed.us/r6/mbs/.

Bus routes: None

• •

T he route of the Iron Goat Trail is best known for two things: for the impressive engineering of the mountainside switch-backs and the Cascade Tunnel, and for the tragedy of 1910, when an avalanche knocked fifteen cars off the rails and killed ninety-six people. The tragedy was but the final blow for the train's passengers, who had been stalled for seven days watching hillsides of rocks, snow, and trees sliding over the tracks.

The drama of the railroad started back in 1891 when engineers like Charles Haskell and John Stevens forced their way to Stevens Pass through challenging terrain and difficult weather. Then came the construction of intricate switchbacks cut into the mountainside. In 1900 the completion of the original 2.6-mile Cascade Tunnel eliminated the tedious use of the switchbacks. Though snowsheds were added to protect trains from avalanches, trains were still halted for days at a time in winter storms. These historic events are documented in the *Iron Goat Trail Guidebook.*

Many of the tunnels are collapsed or covered with slide debris. They can be viewed from the trail, but do not attempt to enter any tunnels or to walk on rotten timbers. Please stay on the trail to protect the wildflowers.

Although you can access the trail from either end, this description begins at the Martin Creek Trailhead. Trains once climbed through a 170-degree horseshoe-shaped tunnel (now collapsed) at Martin Creek, creating an upper and a lower track. The trailhead lies at the elevation of the lower section of the tracks. This is called the lower trail.

For a short, flat hike, take the lower trail to the end at 1.2 miles. Listen for the rustling leaves of hardwood trees as you travel across

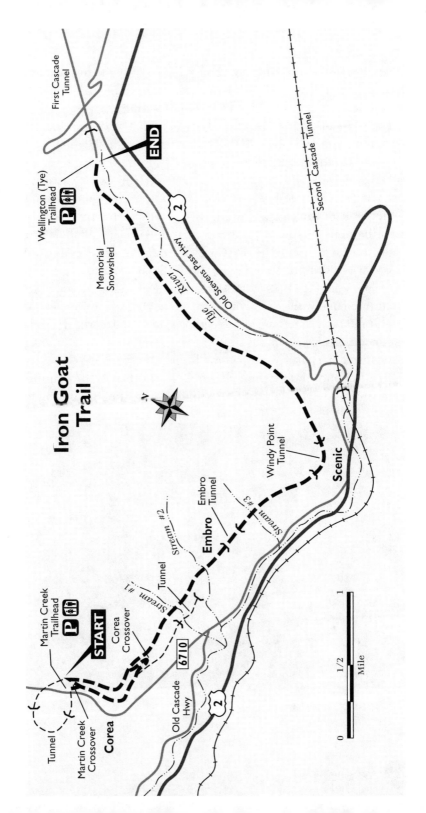

Iron Goat Trail

First Cascade Tunnel

Wellington (Tye) Trailhead P 🏕

Memorial Snowshed

END

2

Tye River

Old Stevens Pass Hwy

Second Cascade Tunnel

N

Windy Point Tunnel

Embro Tunnel

Stream #2

Scenic

Stream #3

Embro

Tunnel

Stream #1

Martin Creek Trailhead P 🏕

START

Corea Crossover

6710

Tunnel

Martin Creek Crossover

Corea

Old Cascade Hwy

2

0   1/2   1
          Mile

Stream #1, to the Twin Tunnels and the 96-foot-high concrete arch of a snowshed. This trail will eventually extend an additional 1.5 miles, ending at a trailhead at the town of Scenic.

For a longer outing from the Martin Creek Trailhead (elevation 2,380 feet), you can take either of two crossover trails (which avoid the collapsed tunnel) up to the upper grade. From the trailhead, the trail crosses wetlands on a boardwalk. The Martin Creek Crossover appears after the boardwalk and takes you up a short, steep trail to the upper trail. You can take this crossover and turn right when you reach the upper grade, or (for a longer trail with less slope) continue on the lower grade to the Corea Crossover at 0.5 mile. This crossover is a third of a mile long; turn right at the top.

At just under 2 miles from Martin Creek, you'll find one of the remaining back walls of eleven massive concrete snowsheds, just before Embro, once the site of a telegraph station and workers' shacks. A spur trail leads you to the spillway and reservoir built to manage fires caused by sparks from passing trains.

Just beyond, follow the spur trail around the Embro Tunnel. From the tunnel's east portal to Windy Point, timber snowsheds

This concrete snowshed was built in 1910–11 at the site of the 1910 Avalanche disaster. (Courtesy Tom Davis, U.S.F.S.)

One of many tunnels and snowshed backwalls along the trail. (Courtesy Ruth Ittner)

combine with the concrete sheds to create a corridor covering this 1-mile section of track.

Arrive at the Windy Point Tunnel at 3 miles. The trail follows the original grade around the tunnel on the edge of the mountainside. Check out the active tunnel below from the viewpoint and follow the trail on the 2-foot-wide ledge of the snowshed archway to view the east portal. Continue east past several snowsheds.

At mile 6 you'll come upon a snowshed that now serves as a memorial to those who died here in the avalanche of 1910. The Wellington depot was built just beyond this point, in 1883. It was moved east when this snowshed was built. A year after the avalanche disaster both the depot and the town of Wellington were renamed Tye: The railroad knew that passengers simply would not want to pass through "Wellington."

Pass a runaway track and cross Haskell Creek to reach the Wellington Trailhead, 3,100 feet in elevation. Continue 0.25 mile to view the west portal of the Cascade Tunnel.

When you're ready, turn around and return the way you came. For a longer outing, consider a drive or an overnight to the town of Leavenworth. Or you might want to visit the rail-trail at Wallace Falls.

12 Cascade Trail

The Cascade Trail reaches into the Cascade foothills in rural northwestern Washington. It parallels Route 20 on the flats until it climbs to a wooded hillside near Concrete. It crosses twenty-three trestles, which range from 10 to 2,200 feet long.

Activities:

Location: Sedro Woolley to Concrete, Skagit County

Length: 23 miles

Surface: Crushed rock and ballast

Wheelchair access: This trail is not wheelchair accessible.

Difficulty: Easy—although the ballast is difficult to ride on a bike in most areas, and equestrian use deteriorates it further.

Food: You'll find things to eat in the towns of Sedro Woolley and Concrete.

Rest rooms: Public rest rooms are available at all trailheads.

Seasons: The trail can be used year-round.

Access and parking: To reach the western trailhead at Sedro Woolley, take I–5 to exit 232 (Cook Road) and turn right. Take a left onto Route 20 and drive several miles to Fruitdale Road. Turn right.

To reach the trail's eastern trailhead, drive Route 20 to Concrete. Turn north into town on E Avenue, then turn right onto Railroad Street and drive to the senior center.

To access the trail at Birdsview turn left off Route 20 onto Baker Lake Road. Horse trailer parking is available at all trailheads.

Rentals: No rentals are available along this route.

Contact:

- Skagit County Parks and Recreation, (360) 336–9414, www.skagitcounty. net/offices/parks/index.htm
- Sedro Woolley Chamber of Commerce, (360) 855–1841, www.sedro-woolley.com
- Concrete Chamber of Commerce, (360) 853–7042, www.concrete-wa.com

Bus route: Skagit Transit #717, (360) 757–4433, www.skat.org

● ●

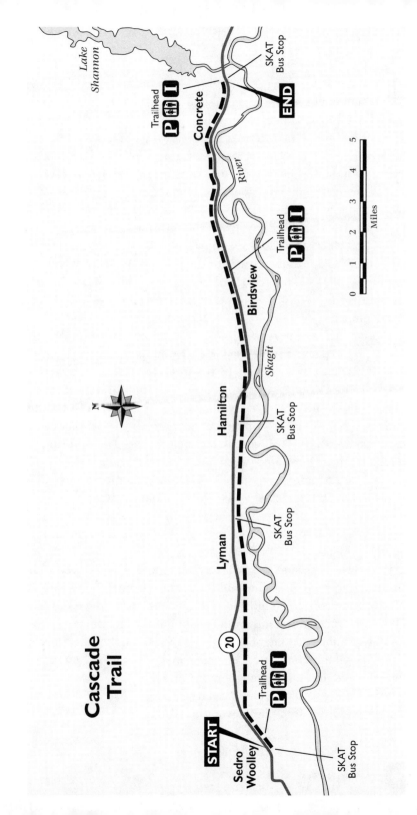

Cascade Trail

START

Sedro Woolley

SKAT Bus Stop

Trailhead P 👥 ℹ

20

Lyman

SKAT Bus Stop

SKAT Bus Stop

Hamilton

Skagit

Birdsview

Trailhead P 👥 ℹ

River

Trailhead P 👥 ℹ

Concrete

Lake Shannon

SKAT Bus Stop

END

N

0   1   2   3   4   5
Miles

The Great Northern Railroad (GNRR) once connected down-river towns with the wooded areas along the upper Skagit where the Cascade Trail now runs. Independent businessmen sought their riches among the forests of cedar trees that filled the valley. In Sedro Woolley, P. A. Woolley made a fortune supplying ties for the GNRR; merchants prospered, too, from the passengers traveling through town. The line transported cement, lumber, and shakes. The town of Concrete shipped cement as far as the Pacific during World War II. The GNRR arrived in town in 1900. The cement plants, opened in 1904 and 1907, supplied the Grand Coulee Dam, Baker River Dam, and Ballard Locks. Eleven miles of the line—from Sedro Woolley to Hamilton—ran freight until 1990. The trail was completed in 1999. The railroad right-of-way extends to Anacortes, where a trail is being developed.

You can access the trail from several points along the way; this description takes you from west to east. The pathway starts on the outskirts of Sedro Woolley among the trees. Mileage is well marked. At mile 7 the Skagit River comes up to the trail for a brief, scenic passage. Three miles out of Lyman, you'll cross Lyman-Hamilton Road; there's a SKAT bus stop here if you're ready to turn back. You'll next cross lots of creeks before reaching Route 20. The trail runs beside the highway here. Just past mile 14, pass Lusk Road. Head south to reach the 120-acre Rasar State Park on the Skagit River. Just down the trail, pull off to the Baker Lake grocery and gas station for an ice cream. Detour onto the bridge walkway on Route 20 to cross Grandy Creek at Baker Lake Road. Return immediately to the trail on Bird-dog Private Lane.

You can ride beside the trail on Challenger Road between Russell Road and mile 19 if you find the surface difficult for a bike. At mile 18, you're on a lush hillside and can begin to see the mountains to the east. Once you spot the unusual building that bridges the road (it's a high school), you're nearing downtown Concrete. Pass the concrete silos where concrete dust was stored, and cross E Avenue to the trail's end at the Concrete Senior Center.

Turn up E Avenue to tour Concrete and get a snack, dinner, or an espresso. You'll find public rest rooms adjacent to the old school-

One of the cascading streams near the eastern edge of the trail. (Courtesy Lou Petersen, Skagit County and Recreation)

house. Built in 1936, it served a population double the 800 residents of today. Cross the historic Thompson Bridge to rest at the riverside picnic tables at the Baker River Fish Facility Visitors Center. This bridge connected the towns of Baker and Cement City in 1918; at the time, it was the longest single-span cement bridge in the world.

Enjoy this little town and ride the bus back to your starting point. But first, take a historic tour on the open-air Sockeye Express bus (360–853–7042).

This trail comes in two parts. A paved trail leaves the city of Snohomish and travels north through farmland, wetlands, and fields; at Lake Stevens the pathway turns to rough dirt and runs through rural and wooded country. Skaters savor the wide, smooth pavement, while equestrians enjoy the soft, 6-foot-wide parallel path. Multiple access points, fun towns, and several parks and lakes contribute to a relaxing day or a weekend getaway.

Activities:

Location: Snohomish, Lake Stevens, and Marysville, all in Snohomish County

Length: 15.75 miles

Surface: 7.25 miles of the trail are asphalt; 8.5 miles are dirt.

Wheelchair access: The paved trail of the first 7.25 miles is wheelchair accessible.

Difficulty: The paved portion of the trail is easy; the dirt section is moderate due to mud and brush.

Food: Snohomish and Lake Stevens have restaurants, espresso shops, and markets within a mile of the trail. Vending machines and covered seating are available at Division Street in Machias.

Rest rooms: The trailheads at the Pilchuck parking area, Bonneville Ballpark, and Division Street have chemical toilets or rest rooms

Seasons: The trail can be used year-round.

Access and parking: The corner of Maple Street and Pine Avenue in Snohomish marks the southern terminus of the trail. Exit I–5 at Route 2 eastbound to Snohomish and Wenatchee, then exit Route 2 at Snohomish. Turn left onto Second Street, then left (north) onto Maple Street, and drive about 1 mile to Pine Avenue. From Route 9, exit at Snohomish and drive north to Second Street. Turn left, then left again at Maple, and proceed to Pine. You can park on the street here.

To reach the other trailheads, drive north on Maple, which becomes Machias Road. The Pilchuck parking area is 1.5 miles up the road, on the right. To reach the Machias Trailhead, continue north on Machias Road to Division Street and turn west; you can park about an eighth of a mile ahead.

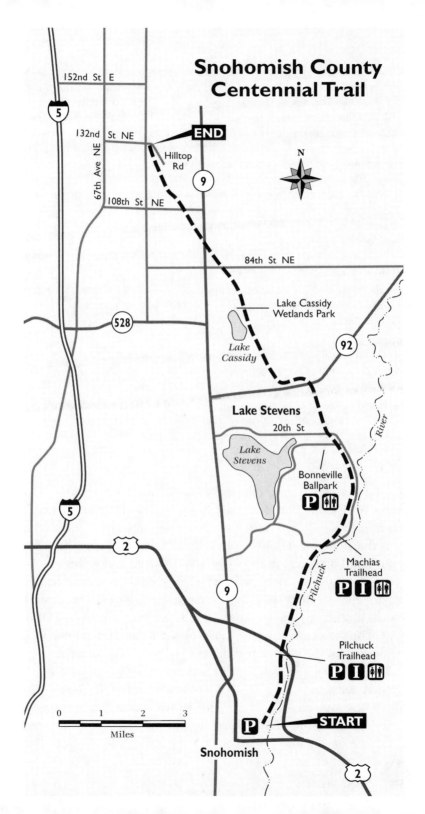

Snohomish County Centennial Trail

152nd St E

132nd St NE

END

Hilltop Rd

67th Ave NE

108th St NE

N

84th St NE

Lake Cassidy Wetlands Park

528

Lake Cassidy

92

Lake Stevens

20th St

Lake Stevens

Bonneville Ballpark

Machias Trailhead

Pilchuck Trailhead

Pilchuck

River

5

5

2

9

9

2

0   1   2   3
Miles

START

Snohomish

Parking for the northern, undeveloped section is found in downtown Lake Stevens and at the Bonneville Ballpark, both of which require a short road ride. The Bonneville Ballpark is located at 16th Street Northeast and North Machias Road. Drive north from Snohomish on Machias Road, or exit Route 9 at Lake Stevens. Drive east from town on Hartford Street. Turn right at the T-intersection (131st Avenue) and left at the next T (16th Street). This park may be gone when 16th Street is widened.

Another option is to park at 12th Avenue and Route 92. This tiny pull-out is planned to be turned into a major trailhead when the northern trail is developed. Finally, you can access the northern trail from 84th Street Northeast. Look for a gravel clearing on both sides of this street; you'll see a sign for the trail.

The Lake Stevens Trail is a 0.75-mile unpaved link on which residents can walk or cycle to the Centennial Trail.

Rentals: None in the area. Bike repairs and accessories are available at Centennial Cycles (360–568–1345) at the Soccer Dome adjacent to the trail on Maple Street.

Contacts:
- Snohomish County Parks and Recreation Department, (425) 388–6600, www.co.snohomish.wa.us/parks
- Group Activities on the Trail, (425) 388–6608

Bus routes: Take bus #210 from Smokey Point to Marysville. For information, call (425) 353–RIDE or (800) 562–1375; TDD (425) 778–2188. Or visit the Web site at www.commtrans.org.

• •

I f the sunny summer crowds of Seattle are not your style, head north. The Snohomish Valley lies 40 miles northeast of Seattle. The valley's hundred-year history of dairying and farming is evident along the Snohomish County Centennial Trail, which begins in Snohomish and presently ends between Marysville and Arlington. Development of the northern portion will extend the paved trail 9 miles. Take the time to enjoy the antiques shops and eateries of Snohomish, along with the tiny town center and the huge Lake Stevens. Or try the trail on the weekend of the Snohomish car show. Downtown roads are closed and the band is playing; it's one very big block party.

The southern 7.25 miles of this trail are peaceful, paved, and well planned. Smooth, wide pavement attracts skaters and a 6-foot-wide soft trail is mowed and brushed for equestrians. The presence of horses and the calm, rural setting take you back to the heyday of the

The northern portion of the trail is still undeveloped.

dairy and farming industries, when this area was served by the Seattle, Lakeshore & Eastern Railroad. Past years of heavy logging have left no scars. Well-placed benches and picnic tables and occasional interpretive and historic signs invite you to stop, look, and imagine. Wheelchair travelers and walkers will enjoy these spots for breaks.

The northern 8.5 miles is undeveloped. It's a rough single-track dirt trail with downed branches, face-slapping alders, and a few lengthy mudholes—a mountain bike adventure. Bring clear glasses along with your sunglasses for face protection, and dry socks. Equestrians will have this secluded area mostly to themselves until it's developed. There are no services along the way. Be prepared.

You can access the trail from many points along the way; this description begins in Snohomish, its southern end, and proceeds northward. From the trailhead at Pine Avenue and Maple Street, take in Snohomish's flower boxes and benches, then begin your journey along the Pilchuck River. Benches and picnic tables are thoughtfully placed for views and serenity—you'll find them at the edge of a field, beside the river, below a bridge, and at a display describing the critters that wander the wetlands and rivers.

The railroad's history, locations of the old train stations, and trail mileage are all listed at the Pilchuck parking lot 1.5 miles up the trail. The Snohomish–Arlington run of the Seattle, Lakeshore & Eastern Railroad's Sumas line came to town in 1889 and continued through the 1950s. In 1989 the rail-trail was planned and named for this hundred-year history. It opened in 1991, with the final mile completed in 1994.

The train came from Woodinville to Snohomish, Arlington, and Bryant—the site of a big mill and a 100-foot-high trestle—through the town of Pilchuck and on to the Canadian border. The Seattle–North Bend run completed the route to Seattle for shipping lumber and carrying mail and livestock. Shingle mills were big business in the railroad's peak years; they required little investment, and the Snohomish Valley had plenty of cedar. Snohomish had four shingle mills, Marysville had seven. You can still see the mill beside the trail in Lake Stevens.

The Machias Trailhead at Division Street, 4 miles up the path, provides a sense of heritage. Rest rooms are housed in the pretty blue replica of a depot built in the late 1890s. The photos of the town of Machias take you back to the early 1900s. Hitch your horse, check out some history, let the kids loose in the grassy area, or snack at the covered picnic tables. At 4.5 miles, just past the Machias cutoff, a kiosk introduces the woodchuck, Pacific salamander, belted kingfisher, great blue heron, and other members of this wetland community.

Head north for a sign that relates some amusing and historic cow tales of the turn of the twentieth century, when "No udder business was better than dairy." You can learn the prolific peculiarities of Miss Sadie and Rose, which led to their local fame. Try to guess how many offspring they had or how much milk they produced in a year before you reach the sign. Farther on, you can learn what swims, flies, and slithers here. Settle in at a pretty spot on the river and find out what a mountain beaver or a northern flicker looks like.

The maintained trail presently ends at 20th Street in Lake Stevens. Turn left here or at the previous crossing at 16th Street. To grab an espresso or a meal, continue 0.25 mile to the old section of town. You'll find a bike shop, a library, a market, two restaurants, some shops, and a community park on the lake itself. Try the lemon meringue pie at the Lakeshore or pizza at the Neapolis.

If you'd like to continue your trek northward on dirt, exit the trail, turn left at 16th Street, take the first right off 16th (131st Avenue) and continue straight for 1 mile. As you cross Brett Road, detour right to see the sign: CITE OF HARTFORD BEGINNING OF HISTORIC RR TO MONTE CRISTO. BUILT 1891–93. This is where the Monte Cristo line branched west to the Stillaguamish River and on to the mines of Monte Cristo, an investment that attracted John D. Rockefeller (and his deep pock-

Equestrians travel the soft path near Pilchuck Trailhead in Snohomish.

Trail users navigate the falling foliage along the paved trailway.

ets). There he built a concentrator that brought supplies to the mines by rail, then took the ore out.

Where the paved road curves left at the Hartford substation, continue straight onto a dirt road. Pass under Route 92. The single-track begins at the end of the paved underpass just across the next street, 12th Avenue. By fall 2001 the trail will go straight through with no road detours. Ride or walk the narrow path, thick with maples and alders, birds fluttering about. Your only clue that you're passing Lake Cassidy is a small trail to the left that empties into a dirt turnaround. The lake and wetland park are beyond. You'll find bass and trout here.

At 4 miles, cross 84th Street Northeast, a main thoroughfare—use caution. Get ready for some serious mud crossings, and beware: The mud is deeper than it looks. You'll cross under Route 9 at about 6 miles, and then under Lauck Road. Streets are named twice in this area: old names and new names. Lauck Road, for instance, is also 108th Street Northeast, while 84th Street Northeast is also Getchell Road. The 911 emergency service needed numbers, and the residents wanted their history. Get some views of valley farms as the trail traverses a ridge. Exit at 8.5 miles at Hilltop Road, through a private driveway. The trail is presently impassable beyond this point. From here you can backtrack down the trail.

If you're on a bike, however, you might want to ride roads and buses back to Lake Stevens. Take a left on Hilltop, then another left at 67th. *Caution:* There are no shoulders on this busy street. The first right (132nd Street) takes you to 51st Street/Schulte Road and north to Arlington or to a bus stop. (Each bus can take two bikes.) The bus will take you south to Marysville, where you'll find food and a bike shop. Bus #260 will take you back to Lake Stevens (there's no service on Sunday, though). Or you might ride east on Fourth Street from downtown Marysville (uphill) to Route 9. Turn right (south), then left onto 60th Street/Lake Cassidy Road. Enjoy Lake Cassidy and the country roads. Pass the county park access to the lake. Turn right on 99th Avenue Northeast and left on Route 92. You'll arrive at the start of the dirt trail on 12th Avenue in 1.5 miles.

Plans to pave the trail were on hold at press time. A key gate will provide handicapped access to Lake Cassidy; the trail and a boardwalk will end at a fishing dock. The final plan will extend the Centennial Trail another 16 miles, through Arlington and north to the Skagit County line. Cyclists will finally have an alternative to Route 9, which has no shoulder north of Arlington. The 44 miles of the Centennial Trail will be complete when it connects with the Snoqualmie Valley Trail (Trail 10) south of Monroe.

The Interurban Electric Trolley motored passengers between Mount Vernon and Bellingham Bay from 1889 to 1903. The trolley route takes you high above Chuckanut Drive and Bellingham Bay, on a path amid evergreens, deciduous trees, and the occasional home. Though Chuckanut Drive is a hilly, curvy street, the trail is quite flat except for one section.

Activities:

Location: Larrabee State Park to Fairhaven, Whatcom County

Length: 7 miles

Surface: Crushed stone; one difficult section has dirt and mud.

Wheelchair access: Fairhaven Park is wheelchair accessible.

Difficulty: Easy in the southern portion and northwest of Arroyo Park; difficult between California Street and Arroyo Park.

Food: You'll find things to eat in Fairhaven.

Rest rooms: All trailheads except Arroyo Park offer both rest rooms and drinking water.

Seasons: The trail can be used year-round.

Access and parking: Follow the signs for Larrabee State Park from exit 250 (Fairhaven Parkway) off I–5. Drive west on Fairhaven Parkway for 1.5 miles to 12th Street.

To start in Fairhaven, turn left into the Rotary Trailhead before you reach 12th or turn into Fairhaven Park on Chuckanut Drive. To reach Larrabee State Park and trailheads on Chuckanut Drive and Old Samish Way, turn left onto 12th Street; after 2 blocks, bear left onto Chuckanut Drive. (Fairhaven Park is on your left.) To reach Arroyo Park, turn left onto Old Samish Way (there's a gallery on your right). The North Chuckanut Mountain Trailhead and California Street are just beyond this turnoff. Cyclists may wish to park here and climb up the steep quarter-mile grade on California Street to avoid the single-track in Arroyo Park. To start at the southern trailhead at Larrabee State Park, stay on Chuckanut Drive, turning left into the Clayton Beach Trailhead 0.5 mile past the main entrance to the park (5 miles from Fairhaven Parkway). You can also park on neighborhood streets and access the trail from there.

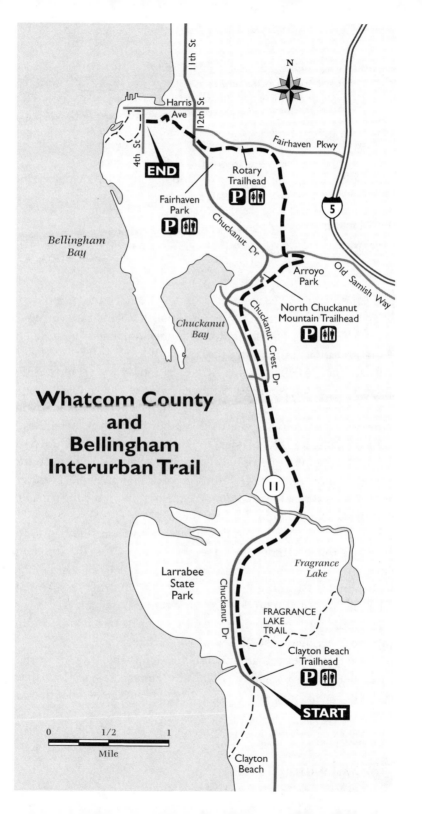

Rentals: Try Fairhaven Bike & Mountain Sports at 1103 11th Street, (360) 733–4433, www.fairhavenbike.com; Jack's Bicycle Center at 1907 Iowa Street, (360) 733–1955; or Baker Bike & Board at 209 East Holly, (360) 733–3728.

Contacts:
- City of Bellingham Parks and Recreation, (360) 676–6985, www.cob. org/parks.htm
- Whatcom County Parks and Recreation, (360) 733–2900
- Bellingham/Whatcom County Convention and Visitors Bureau, (360) 671–3990, www.bellingham.com
- Fairhaven Association, (360) 738–1574 (for merchant and historical information)

Bus route: Contact the Whatcom Transit Authority (WTA), (360) 676–RIDE.

· ·

In 1915, the Larrabee and Gates families donated the twenty acres that became Larrabee State Park, the first state park in Washington. The park's Chuckanut Mountain includes a network of signed hiking and mountain biking pathways that take off from the Interurban Trail. To explore these trails, purchase the "Happy Trails" map at Village Books on 11th Street.

You can park your car and access the trail from many points along its way; this description begins at its southern end, the Clayton Beach Trailhead. Look for the trail sign at the northwest corner of the parking lot. Once you're on this short access trail, take a right to continue on the Interurban Trail. (From the parking lot, about 3 miles of flat trail stretch northward; you have the option of turning back at a difficult section or continuing on to Fairhaven.)

You can also head left at this intersection for a side trip to the beach on a rugged, undeveloped section of trail. Cross the street and follow the trail over logs and through brush to reach the water's edge. The Burlington Northern Railroad may grant rights to Larrabee State Park to develop and maintain this access to Bellingham Bay.

Heading north on the main trail, you'll run into hikers coming from the Fragrance Lake Trailhead at 0.5 mile.

The forest of second-growth and deciduous trees begins to open up to a view of the bay and the islands in 2 miles. Cross several streets and meet Chuckanut Drive where it rises up to the level of the trail at Chuckanut Crest Drive. If you want to avoid steep hills, exit the trail to a second car parked on the road here or turn back.

After this brief encounter with civilization, you'll reach a couple of hills and then a drop to a sudden stop sign at California Street at 4.5 miles. Cyclists have two choices. One option is to turn left onto California, then right onto Chuckanut Drive to Old Samish Highway for a roadside detour of about a mile. Turn right and regain the trail across the street from the Arroyo Park lot. Climb up the steps to the flat trail to continue to Fairhaven.

If you're looking for a forest hike or a single-track route accented by a couple of sharp switchbacks and steep hills on a narrow, muddy trail, however, the second option is just your ticket. Continue across California to the trail. Take the right fork and head into a deep mossy forest crossed by creeks and bridges, decorated by a small waterfall, and orchestrated by Chuckanut Creek.

When all this fun is done, stop to enjoy the sounds and smells of Chuckanut Creek and the forest as you cross the long wooden bridge. Turn left at the trail across the bridge for an uphill haul to Samish Way, a parking area, and the trail. Cross Samish Way and climb the steps up to the flat trail. The pilings from the large trestle that once crossed here now support a bench for trail users. (This is where you arrive if you take a left on California to avoid the park.) Head into a pleasant, more open area on the fringes of town. Cross several small streets and parallel Fairhaven Parkway.

You'll cross 20th Street 1 mile from the Arroyo Park Trailhead. Head straight, following the yellow-striped brown posts on the sidewalk beside Julia Street. The trail heads right as the street curves left. Pass the Rotary Trailhead on your right and leave the neighborhood to enter the wooded Padden Creek area. You'll reach Donovan Avenue and 10th Street at Padden Creek less than 1 mile from the Rotary Trailhead. You can turn onto 10th Street to head into Fairhaven, and to reach the South Bay Trail (Trail 15).

To wind around the bay for a mile before returning to Fairhaven and to the South Bay Trail, continue on the trail beside Padden Creek. Cross Sixth Street and wind down around the wastewater plant to a trail paralleling the waterfront. This is a doggy play area, with bags for waste disposal available at the trailhead to your right. Turn left for a 0.2-mile detour to the active rail and some secluded waterfront. Turn right to the wastewater parking lot and onto Fourth Street. Turn left onto Harris Avenue. (This is more or less a dead end—there's only one way to go.) Take a moment to smell the coffee—Starbucks is straight ahead at the ferry terminal.

Or you can turn right onto Harris and then left at 10th, which dead-ends at the South Bay Trail in 1 block—about 0.6 mile from Starbucks. For a reading and feasting treat, head up to 11th Street and turn right to rest at Village Books and the Colophon Café. African peanut soup, espresso, and Moosetracks ice cream sound good?

15 South Bay Trail

Read about local history, see a sunset, walk the waterfront, pass through a park, and enjoy the shops and eateries of downtown Bellingham. Starting at Fairhaven most of the South Bay Trail hugs the shore of Bellingham Bay.

Activities:

Location: Bellingham, Whatcom County

Length: 2 miles

Surface: Asphalt, crushed stone, concrete

Wheelchair access: Boulevard Park is wheelchair accessible.

Difficulty: Easy, except for climbing some steps, descending several hills, and a railroad crossing or two.

Food: You can stock up in downtown Bellingham and Fairhaven.

Rest rooms: There are rest rooms and drinking water at Boulevard Park.

Seasons: The trail can be used year round.

Access and parking: Take exit 250 (Fairhaven Parkway) off I–5, then drive west on Fairhaven for 1.5 miles to 12th Street. Turn right, then left in 4 blocks onto Mill Avenue. It dead-ends at the trailhead on 10th Street. You can park on the street.

South State Street has several pullouts; steps lead down to the trail for an evening stroll. To reach South State Street, continue on 12th. It becomes Finnegan Way, then 11th, and then State.

Boulevard Park (midtrail) can be reached from Bayview Drive off of South State Street. This is a nice spot for a quick trip south along the prettiest portion of the trail. The northern terminus is downtown at East Maple Street west of Railroad Avenue; you can park on the street to access the trail.

Rentals: Try Fairhaven Bike & Mountain Sports at 1103 11th Street, (360) 733–4433, www.fairhavenbike.com; Jack's Bicycle Center at 1907 Iowa Street, (360) 733–1955; or Baker Bike & Board, 209 East Holly, (360) 733–3728.

Contacts: City of Bellingham Parks and Recreation, (360) 676–6985, www.cob.org/parks.htm; or Bellingham/Whatcom County Convention and Visitors Bureau, (360) 671–3990, www.bellingham.com.

Bus route: Contact the Whatcom Transit Authority, (360) 676–RIDE.

• •

This line of the Bellingham Bay and Eastern Railway once pulled coal, sawlogs, and lumber from the Lake Whatcom watershed to ship to developing West Coast cities. The first mill in the area—Henry Roeder's Mill—was built in 1850, and there were no fewer than sixty-eight shingle mills in Whatcom County by 1900. The largest mill in the world, the Puget Sound Sawmill and Timber Company, operated in Fairhaven.

You can park your car and access the right-of-way—now the South Bay Trail—from many spots along its way. This description takes you from its southern terminus, 10th Street and Mill Avenue, northward. As you head north, the trail takes you onto 10th briefly until it descends some steps at a trail marker at Easton Avenue. You'll cross the tracks and hike up some steps, only to drop down even more steps to the water. Cross a lovely boardwalk and enter Boulevard Park at 0.2 mile from the steps.

For an alternate bike route that bypasses the steps, continue north on 10th. Travel 1 block on State Street/11th and turn left at Bayview into Boulevard Park—a great spot for sunsets.

The interpretive signs along the trail are interesting and fun, especially when combined with a historic tour of Fairhaven. Cross the tracks (carefully) at the north end of Boulevard Park to continue north, or hike up the steps to the overpass. The paved trail takes you past pulp mills and other industries until you reach East Maple Street, where the trail ends.

If you'd like to extend your trek, you have many options. Turn right onto Railroad Avenue and left to pass the brewery, the Great Adventure outdoor store, restaurants, and cafes. You can also cross Maple and continue straight into the alley for an alternate bike route. Consider taking one of four historic reproduction trolley cars back to Fairhaven.

A mile and a half on city streets will take you to the Railroad Trail (Trail 16). Turn right off Railroad onto York and left onto State. State becomes James Street. Turn right on East North Street (1 block north of the light at Alabama) and left at the T-intersection onto King Street to find the trailhead on your right.

If you're traveling southbound on the South Bay Trail, you can connect with the Interurban Trail (Trail 14). From 10th and Mill, turn

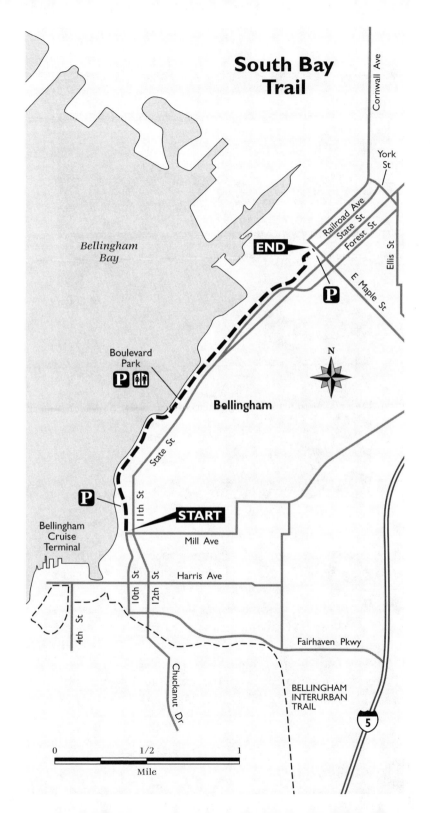

South Bay Trail

Bellingham Bay

END

START

Boulevard Park

Bellingham

Bellingham Cruise Terminal

Cornwall Ave

York St

Railroad Ave

State St

Forest St

Ellis St

E Maple St

N

State St

11th St

Mill Ave

10th St

12th St

Harris Ave

4th St

Chuckanut Dr

Fairhaven Pkwy

BELLINGHAM INTERURBAN TRAIL

5

0   1/2   1
Mile

South Bay Trail near Fairhaven.

right onto Harris Avenue and left onto Fourth Street. Turn right into the wastewater plant parking lot. The trail begins at the doggy poop stand.

Whale-watching tours and ferries to the San Juan Islands, Victoria, and Alaska leave from the Bellingham Cruise Terminal at Fourth and Harris. A nearby boat launch is convenient for kayaking, sailing, and pleasure boating. Rentals are available.

The city and county consider these trails to be works in progress. Some signage is missing. Links have been proposed to connect the trails and create a better route through the city.

16 Railroad Trail

The Railroad Trail leaves Bellingham to make a gradual climb through quiet neighborhoods and Whatcom Falls State Park. (If you prefer to head downhill, start from the park.) The trail is lightly wooded for most of its length. Though the park isn't large, pay attention: The network of trails can get you off track. You might enjoy a planned detour to the creekside; picnic facilities are available at both Whatcom Falls and Bloedel-Donovan Parks, while the former has a kids' fishing pond and hatchery.

Activities:

Location: Bellingham, Whatcom County

Length: 3.5 miles

Surface: Crushed stone; some gravel and dirt areas

Wheelchair access: The trail's only wheelchair access is found at Whatcom Falls Park and Bloedel-Donovan Park.

Difficulty: Easy to moderate. Traveling from west to east, the trail offers a gradual uphill grade with some moderate slopes.

Food: Bloedel-Donovan Park (seasonal) and Barkley Village Shopping Center on Woburn Street offer things to eat.

Rest rooms: There are rest rooms and drinking water at Bloedel-Donovan and Whatcom Falls Parks.

Seasons: The trail can be used year-round.

Access and parking: To reach the western trailhead near Memorial Park, get off I–5 at Sunset Drive (exit 255). From I–5 southbound, go straight, down James Street. From I–5 northbound, turn left onto Sunset to cross the highway, then turn left onto James. After several blocks, turn left onto North Street, then left again onto King Street. The trailhead is on your right.

Find the eastern trailhead by turning east onto Sunset Drive/Mount Baker Highway, south (right) onto Orleans Street, and east (left) onto Alabama Street. Turn right onto Electric Avenue at Lake Whatcom. The trailhead is immediately on your right.

Rentals: Try Fairhaven Bike & Mountain Sports at 1103 11th Street, (360) 733–4433, www.fairhavenbike.com; Jack's Bicycle Center at 1907 Iowa Street, (360) 733–1955; or Baker Bike & Board, 209 East Holly, (360) 733–3728.

Contacts:

- City of Bellingham Parks and Recreation, (360) 676–6985, www.cob.org/parks.htm
- Whatcom County Parks and Recreation, (360) 733–2900
- Bellingham/Whatcom County Convention and Visitors Bureau, (360) 671–3990, www.bellingham.com

Bus route: Contact the Whatcom Transit Authority, (360) 676–RIDE.

• •

You can travel the Railroad Trail in either direction; this description takes you from west to east. Starting from King Street, the trail crosses I–5 and enters a quiet neighborhood with several streets to cross. There is a nice buffer between the small homes and the trail. Cross Woburn Street at 0.9 mile. Get ready for a Pacific Northwest moment: A well-used side trail lures you to the Starbucks at Barkley Village. From here on, pedal hard and burn calories. You'll want to stop here on your way back to chow down. You can create your own smorgasbord of salads, Chinese food, pizza, and other prepared foods at Haagens grocery store and cafe, or choose from a variety of restaurants.

Food fantasies behind you for the moment, push on to pass some pilings from an old trestle. In years past the Bellingham Bay & East-

Remnants of a trestle on the path near Lake Whatcom.

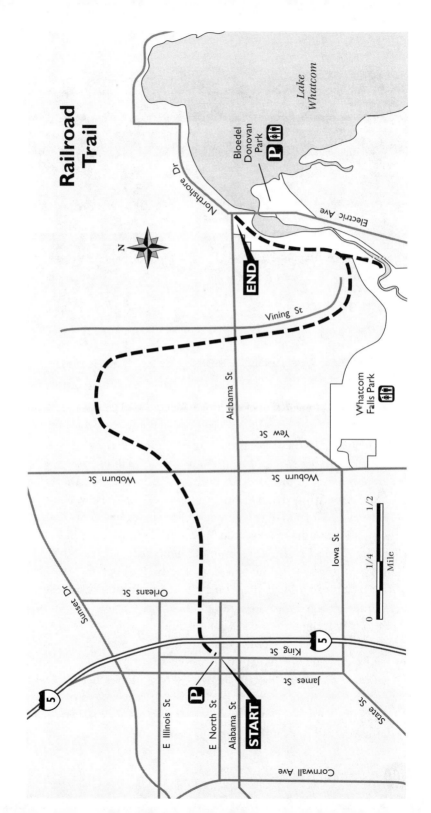

Railroad Trail

N

Lake Whatcom

Bloedel Donovan Park

P

Electric Ave

Northshore Dr

END

Vining St

Alabama St

Yew St

Whatcom Falls Park

Woburn St

Woburn St

Iowa St

Orleans St

Sunset Dr

King St

James St

State St

E Illinois St

E North St

Alabama St

P

START

Cornwall Ave

5

5

0   1/4   1/2
        Mile

Cyclists near the duck pond on the Railroad Trail.

ern Railway occupied the Railroad Trail for 4 miles from New Whatcom to Lake Whatcom. In 1882 the Blue Canyon Mines used the railway to send coal to bunkers on Bellingham Bay. Later, the tracks
brought lumber from Lake Whatcom to the docks of New Whatcom
and Fairhaven for transport to developing western cities, such as San
Francisco. Remnants of trestles can be found along the trail to Lake
Whatcom, around Lake Whatcom, and even across Lake Whatcom.
The BB&E merged with the Northern Pacific Railroad in 1903.

Just past these pilings, head up a hill to an opening beside a pond
at 1.4 miles. A bench provided here makes this a peaceful spot from
which to watch the ducks, the walkers, and the cyclists. As the trail
curves north beyond the pond, take in views of town and the bay below. Steps lead you down to a major street crossing at Alabama Street
at 2 miles. Use caution. Regain the trail across Alabama. A brief narrow dirt trail parallels Vining Street before it heads up a short steeper
hill into Whatcom Falls Park. Turn left at the fork (2.9 miles) to stay
on the main trail. It ends in 0.5 mile.

To catch a glimpse of an old trestle crossing, head straight for a few hundred yards before taking the left fork. You'll see a trail to the right heading downhill before you reach the edge where the trestle lay. You can take a side trip and explore the park and the creek on this trail. (You'll appreciate having a mountain bike.) Turn right at the T-intersection with a wide trail, and then turn left at the first trail *without* steps (the second left). The narrow trail takes you down and across the bridge over Whatcom Creek. Wander around to find a view of the little waterfall below the bridge. Turn left after the bridge. The trail curves around the creek, past a trestle and a kayak practice area. It ends at a small road. Turn right to cross Electric Avenue. Continue on a short trail to the left into Bloedel-Donovan Park, then through the park to Alabama. Find the eastern trailhead at the corner.

Turn around and return the way you came. The trip back is downhill. Bear right when you reach the first fork at mile 0.5. And don't forget Barkley Plaza at mile 2.37. After crossing Woburn, you've got 0.9 mile to the western trailhead at King Street near I–5. There's enough of a grade to cruise happily downhill. Beware of pedestrians.

17 Wallace Falls Railway Trail

On this trek you'll head uphill on a railroad grade for 2.5 miles. Then a 1.5-mile ascent continues on a narrow walking trail up steep switchbacks, through deep woods, and over wooden bridges to spectacular views of Wallace Falls. Get ready for a great workout while you enjoy a rural road trip and a scenic trail with the convenience of camping and the proximity of good food.

Activities:

Location: Wallace Falls State Park, town of Gold Bar, Snohomish County

Length: 2.5 miles. An additional 1.5-mile hiking trail takes you to the waterfalls. A 4.75-mile side trail takes you to Wallace Lake.

Surface: Dirt, somewhat rocky

Wheelchair access: This trail is not wheelchair accessible.

Difficulty: The rail trail is moderate; the hiking trail to the falls is steep.

Food: You'll find restaurants, grocery stores, bakeries, and espresso shops in Gold Bar and other towns along Route 2. Also check out the historic Bush House in Index, and the Sultan Bakery.

Rest rooms: There are bathrooms and water at the trailhead.

Seasons: The trail can be used year-round, but it's closed on Monday and Tuesday from October through April.

Access and parking: Access the trail from Wallace Falls State Park. To reach this park, take Route 2 to Gold Bar, 30 miles east of Everett. Follow signs to the park for 2 miles: You'll turn north onto First Avenue at the park sign and drive 0.5 mile, taking the second right at Huston Street. The trailhead is adjacent to the rest rooms in the parking lot.

Rentals: No rentals are available along this trail.

Contact: Wallace Falls State Park, (360) 793–0420, www.parks.wa.gov/wallacef.htm

Bus routes: None

* *

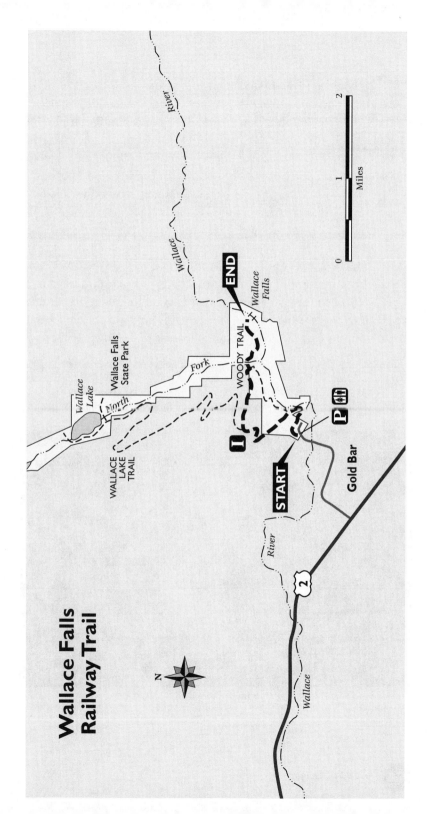

The Wallace River rushes, plummets, and jams up against large river boulders along its course. Nine waterfalls, ranging in height from 50 to 265 feet, plunge into the river from tributaries along its walls, while the waterway itself drops 800 feet in half a mile. Wallace Falls State Park, the site of this riverside trek, is located near several small towns in the Cascade foothills, in Gold Bar off Route 2.

The trail runs along one of several logging railroad routes built in these hills. The railroad grade is steeper than most rail-trails because it was built for wood-fired trains known as steam donkeys, which reached high into the hills after timber. Indeed, it was the invention of the steam donkey and the arrival of the Great Northern Transcontinental Railroad in 1882 that put Gold Bar on the map as a "great northern town." The timing was good, because the increasing number of gravel bars in the Skykomish River was making steamboat travel more and more difficult. Success of the logging industry here then became a sure thing when Frederick Weyerhauser bought 900,000 acres of land from J. J. Hill, Great Northern's owner. The logs were taken to a nearby mill and shipped out from the depot at Gold Bar.

The narrow walking trail meanders through deep woods to spectacular views of the falls.

Washington State eventually purchased the park site from the Weyerhauser timber company; the park opened in 1977. It was built through the efforts of the Youth Development and Conservation Corps programs, thanks to the legislative initiative of Senator Frank Woody, for whom the Woody Trail is named.

Find the trailhead near the parking lot. After 0.25 mile, the trail forks. To your right is the Woody Trail, which departs here to hug the river for 1.5 miles. Stay left to continue on the railroad right-of-way. The surface is good for mountain biking.

Stop to examine the mosaic of the bright green, fuzzy moss that carpets each branch of the forest and each stump top in pleasing designs. You'll hear the distant sound of the river as you climb through the woods on broad switchbacks. If you're lucky, you might see some wildlife. It's not only birds and deer that roam here: This area is also home to coyotes, bobcats, bears, and cougars.

The steam donkey was a wood-fired engine with a wire rope winch mounted on a log sled. When anchored to a stump, it could pull logs out of the woods to a loading site. Unfortunately this "ultimate technological triumph" sent logs flying through the air almost as often as it dragged them across the ground, resulting in numerous injuries and deaths. This precipitated the first phone in the Wallace Falls area—that line between the doctor in Sultan and the logging camps of the Gold Bar Lumber Company and the Wallace Lumber and Manufacturing Company.

At 1.5 miles you'll arrive at the intersection with the Wallace Lake Trail, which departs on your left. There's a kiosk and a picnic table here. Look back through the forest at the old railroad pilings.

Two trails beyond this intersection cut down to the Woody Trail. The right-of-way continues to the North Fork of the Wallace River, where it once crossed on a trestle. Use caution: Steep banks and a steeply dropping river prohibit a safe crossing. Enjoy the view and backtrack to the cutoff down to the river. If you're riding, secure your bike and continue on foot.

Turn left when you reach the river. A bridge crosses the North

Fork here, and the trail climbs to the falls. Steps are built into some
of the steeper portions. Benches are placed along the way—some,
thoughtfully, between switchbacks. Signage is good.

The riverside picnic shelter is your first viewpoint, 0.3 mile from
the bridge. Less than a quarter mile ahead is a dramatic view of Wallace Falls. The trail steepens progressively into shorter switchbacks
over the next 0.5 mile until you reach the upper falls viewpoint at
1,700 vertical feet. One of the logging camps in this area was at 1,800
feet. After your trek uphill, imagine the intense life lived by a log-
ger and his steam donkey in this spot 100 years ago.

Enjoy the mountains peeking through the trees on your descent.
You'll deserve the crème brûlée or the chocolate cheesecake created
by the pastry chef at the Sultan Bakery or dinner at the historic Bush
House, even if you didn't haul a single tree down with you.

Leave Route 101 to tour a pathway with wildflowers, a covered bridge, and a beautifully restored trestle. This segment of the Olympic Discovery Trail offers a combination of flat and rolling terrain with some steep hills.

Activities:

Location: Clallam County, east of Port Angeles

Length: 5 miles

Surface: Packed granite with a brief asphalt section

Wheelchair access: Available at the Morse Creek Trestle only.

Difficulty: Moderate

Food: C'est Si Bon on Cedar Park Drive

Rest rooms: There are no rest rooms along the trail

Seasons. The trail can be used year-round.

Access and parking: The western trailhead lies 4 miles east of Port Angeles. Turn north off Route 101 onto Buchanan Drive, just west of Deer Park Cinemas. Turn left onto Cedar Park Drive and take the second left, signed SCENIC OVERVIEW AHEAD, to the lot.

To reach the Siebert Creek Trailhead, take Old Olympic Highway 1.5 miles to Wild Currant Way. Until the Siebert Creek Bridge is completed, you'll have to reach the trail via the street and a right turn back onto the highway. Cross over the creek and look for the trail on your right.

Rentals: Try Beckett's at 117 West 1st Street (360–452–0842) or Sound Bikes and Kayaks at 120 East Front Street (360–457–1240), both are in Port Angeles.

Contact: Clallam County Roads, (360) 417–2290; or Port Angeles Visitor Center (877) 456–8372, www.cityofpa.com

Ferries: For information, call (800) 843–3779 or visit www.wsdot.wa.gov/ferries/current/.

Bus routes: None

The Olympic Discovery Trail is planned to eventually connect Forks with Port Angeles, Sequim, and Port Townsend. Sections of the trail run on old railroad rights-of-way. The completed trail segments lie in Port Angeles and several miles east of Port Angeles; see Trail 19 for another segment of this ambitious rail-trail.

The Seattle, Port Angeles & Western Railway Company purchased the Seattle, Port Angeles & Lake Crescent Railway Company (1911–15) in 1916, then sold it to the Chicago, Milwaukee & St. Paul in 1918. Two round trips a day reached Discovery Junction from Majestic, with connections to Port Townsend and Seattle. The line to Twin Rivers, west of Port Angeles, was built for logging; in the industry's glory days, three large logging concerns competed to bring a million board feet of logs to the trains each day for shipment to the Orient. As the trees disappeared, the rail line was abandoned. The current rail-trail moves on and off the right-of-way to avoid private property. Be sure to check out the old No. 4 locomotive on Larridsen Boulevard.

Although you can access this segment of the Olympic Discovery Trail from either end, this description begins from its western terminus at Morse Creek. Begin by exploring a brief section of trail to the west of the parking lot. The trail skirts the lot, just below it. Head west down a steep hill to cross Strait View Drive and then the Morse Creek Trestle, built in 1915. The fully decked and railed trestle curves under a maple canopy and over Morse Creek. The trail ends a third of a mile from the road and just over a mile from the parking lot.

Return to the parking lot, and this time head east, following the yellow stripes. Turn left with the road and right onto Cedar Park Drive to the T-intersection at Buchanan. You're backtracking on the route you took to drive to the lot. The crosswalk takes you across to the trail gate. Travel beside Route 101 briefly until the trail turns left at a second gate, just ahead.

Enjoy a brief paved section of trail down a steep hill to the covered bridge, formerly a Bainbridge ferry ramp. You can smell the moisture of the forested ravine. The paved trail ends 0.4 mile from the gate at Route 101, after climbing a steep hill. Once you've moved away from the highway, you'll hear birds chirping and see yellow,

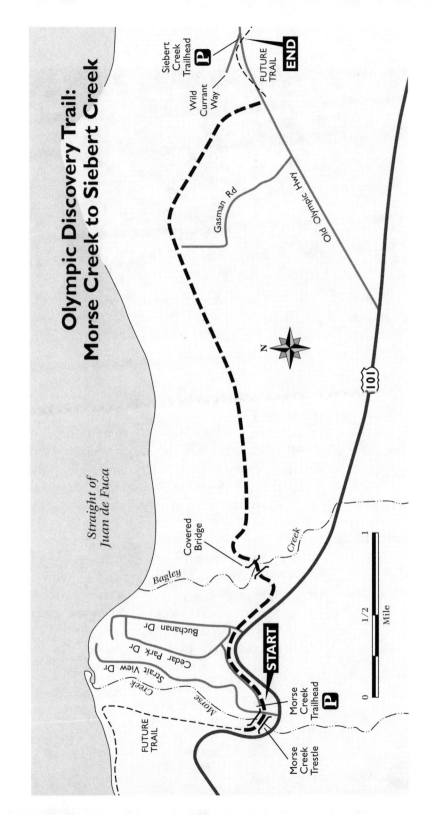

Olympic Discovery Trail: Morse Creek to Siebert Creek

Straight of Juan de Fuca

Siebert Creek Trailhead

P

Wild Currant Way

FUTURE TRAIL

END

Gasman Rd

Old Olympic Hwy

N

101

Covered Bridge

Creek

Bagley

Buchanan Dr

Cedar Park Dr

Strait View Dr

Morse Creek

START

Morse Creek Trailhead

P

FUTURE TRAIL

Morse Creek Trestle

0   1/2   1
Mile

The covered bridge over Bagley Creek.

violet, and white wildflowers. A few cedar trees provide a green background in this open country.

The trail zigzags across a dirt road at 0.9 mile from the gate and again at 1.3 miles. See bright red berries and horses beside the trail. Be prepared for barking dogs at mile 2.3. You'll come to a barrier at mile 3.5; fork right and reach the trail's end at mile 3.7, on Old Olympic Highway. Turn around and return the way you came.

Future Plans

The Siebert Creek Trail Bridge, the 3-mile link from Morse Creek to the Port Angeles Waterfront Trail, and the paving of the trail from Siebert Creek and Old Olympic Highway to Gasman Road will all begin in 2001. The western trailhead will expand to include more parking, rest rooms, and an information center. Other trail segments will be constructed over the next several years.

19 Olympic Discovery Trail: Port Angeles Waterfront

What better place to tour Washington State's coast than on the turbulent Strait of Juan de Fuca? Especially when you can also see Victoria in front of you and the Olympic Mountain Range behind you. This stretch of the Olympic Discovery Trail also lets you stroll along the downtown waterfront, through lumber holding areas, and past an active mill.

Activities:

Location: City of Port Angeles on the Olympic Peninsula, Clallam County

Length: 5 miles

Surface: Asphalt

Wheelchair access: The entire trail is wheelchair accessible, although the trail runs on the roadside at Ediz Hook.

Difficulty: Easy

Food: According to locals, the best fish-and-chips in the world can be found at The Landing at the ferry dock along the trail. There's good Italian food at Bella Italia, and fine Thai food at the Thai Pepper, both a few blocks from the trail. There are wineries and many other restaurants in and near town.

Rest rooms: You'll find rest rooms at the Marina on Marine Drive, at the tip of Ediz Hook, and at the City Pier.

Seasons: The trail can be used year-round.

Access and parking: To start at the City Pier, follow Route 101 into Port Angeles. It will become Front Street. At the intersection with Lincoln Street, turn north onto Lincoln, then drive 1 block to the waterfront and pier. You can also park at the tip of Ediz Hook (the spit), or in downtown Port Angeles; there's street lighting along Marine Drive.

Rentals: Try Beckett's at 117 West 1st Street (360–452–0842) or Sound Bikes and Kayaks at 120 East Front Street (360–457–1240), both are in Port Angeles.

Contact: Port Angeles Chamber of Commerce and Visitor Center, (360) 452–2363, www.cityofpa.com

Ferries: For information, call (800) 843–3779 or visit www.wsdot.wa.gov/
ferries/current/.

Bus routes: None

. . . .

P ort Angeles is the largest city on the northern Olympic Peninsula, headquarters for the Olympic National Park, and site of
the ferry dock for Vancouver Island. The Waterfront Trail here is one
of three open sections of the Olympic Discovery Trail, which is
planned to eventually reach from Forks to Port Townsend. Picnic tables are scattered along the trail, both in town and on the hook. You'll
find the pathway lit at night from the Marina east.

An ideal spot to start your trip is at the City Pier, on Railroad Avenue near Lincoln Street. Here you'll find a lookout tower and the
Art Fiero Marine Lab. Take a free tour of the U.S. Coast Guard cut-
ter *Active* from 1:00 to 4:00 P.M. on weekends and holidays when it's
in town.

The trail stretches eastward for about 0.5 mile. This section is
very serene; you'll find benches and interpretive signs and no city
life.

View of Port Angeles Waterfront from Ediz Hook.

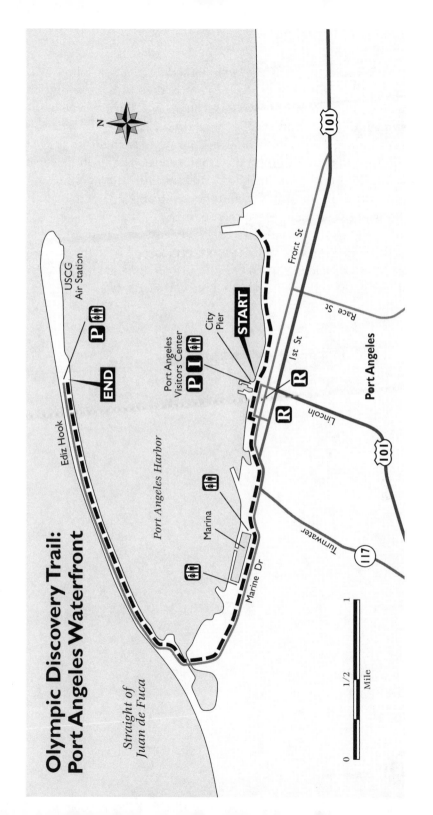

Olympic Discovery Trail: Port Angeles Waterfront

Straight of Juan de Fuca

Port Angeles Harbor

Ediz Hook

USCG Air Station

Marina

Marine Dr

Port Angeles Visitors Center

City Pier

END

START

Front St

Race St

1st St

Lincoln

Turnwater

Port Angeles

101

117

N

0   1/2   1
        Mile

To the west, the trail is a well-marked sidewalk. It follows Railroad Avenue, turns ninety degrees south, then turns west onto the sidewalk beside Marine Drive. Pass the marina, ducks, and a host of fishing boats. The trail sneaks into a little park and on toward the mill, an impressive operation. The pathway is a shoulder on the road from here to the tip of the spit, about 3 miles. Use caution. Check out the ships docked in the harbor and traveling through the strait, with Canada in the distance and the snowcapped Olympic Mountains above. The trail ends at the Coast Guard station.

For the grand coastal tour, continue west on Route 101 to visit rail-trails in Raymond/South Bend (Trail 23) and Astoria, Oregon (Trail 29). Or head north from Keystone to Bellingham for some rail-trail tours through town and in scenic outlying areas.

This fun single-track trail runs along the shores of Lake Crescent in Olympic National Park. It's bounded by steep slate walls above and the water below. Check out a tiny "hole in the rock" tunnel and, after your workout, relax beside mountains reflecting in the turquoise lake.

Activities:

Location: Olympic National Park, 16 miles west of Port Angeles on the Olympic Peninsula, Clallam County

Length: 4 miles

Surface: Smooth dirt and gravel with some rocky areas. Most of the trail is 3 to 4 feet wide, although it has eroded to 2 feet and is banked toward the lake in places.

Wheelchair access: This trail is not wheelchair accessible.

Difficulty: Easy to moderate for walkers; moderate to difficult for bikers.

Food: You'll find many restaurants in Port Angeles (see Trail 19). And in summer only, try the Fairholm General Store on I–101 at Camp David Jr. Road, the Log Cabin Resort near the eastern trailhead, and Lake Crescent Lodge on I–101.

Rest rooms: There is a vault toilet at both trailheads. There is also a toilet above the trail in the woods at the western end of the trail. You'll find flush toilets and water at Fairholm Campground, 4.5 miles from the western trailhead, open May through September.

Seasons: The trail can be used year-round. At only 800 feet in elevation, snow usually isn't a problem. You may find that I–101 west of the trail has some icy hills when the snow level is low. Most services in the area are open May through September.

Access and parking: Take a ferry from Seattle, Edmonds, or Keystone to the Olympic Peninsula and drive to Port Angeles. Take I–101 west from town for 16 miles, then turn right (northwest) onto East Beach Road. Follow the signs to the Log Cabin Resort (accommodations are available here), turning left after 3.3 miles at the trail sign. You'll reach the trailhead 0.8 mile beyond. This road is paved except for the final quarter mile.

You can also access the trail from the west. Turn left off I–101 at Camp David Jr. Road. This paved road ends 0.6 mile later at the Fairholm Campground (eighty-eight sites for tents and RVs). Continue for 4.1 miles on a dirt road to reach the western trailhead; depending on the season and maintenance, this road may be rough.

Rentals: Try Beckett's at 117 West 1st Street (360–452–0842) or Sound Bikes and Kayaks at 120 East Front Street (360–457–1240), both are in Port Angeles.

Contact:

- Olympic National Park Visitors Center is open 9–4. Call (360) 565–3130; for TDD, call (360) 452–0306; for twenty-four-hour recorded information, call (360) 565–3131.
- The Storm King Ranger Station can be reached at (360) 928–3380 or www.nps.gov/olym.
- For fishing regulations, contact the Department of Fish and Wildlife at (360) 902–2200.

Ferries: For information, call (800) 843–3779 or visit www.wsdot.wa.gov/ferries/current/.

Bus routes: None.

• •

The Spruce Railway was a war effort during World War I, when the army needed the light, strong wood of the Sitka spruce to build airplane frames. This tree grows only along the Pacific coastal region from northern California to Alaska, with vast stands located in the roadless Olympic Peninsula. The Army's Spruce Production Division thus built the Olympic Spruce Railroad #1 around Lake Crescent in 1918. Armistice Day arrived on November 11, 1918; nineteen days later, the line was completed. The army sold the railway before a single log had been hauled. It was used for commercial logging until 1954, when it was abandoned. The current 4-mile rail-trail was completed in 1981.

For more information about this trail or the national park itself, stop at the Olympic National Park Visitors Center on Race Street, a short distance east from I–101, in Port Angeles. It's fully accessible and contains a lowland forest display along with information on the natural and cultural history of the park. The park is designated a Man and Biosphere Reserve and a World Heritage Park. Pets are allowed only in parking areas and campgrounds.

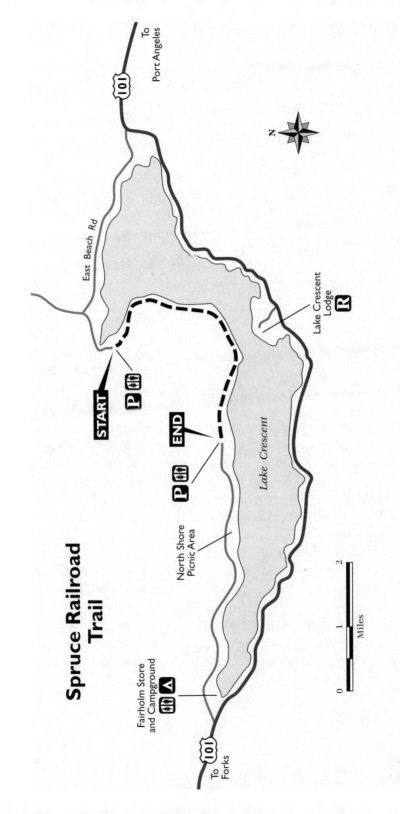

Spruce Railroad Trail

To Port Angeles

101

N

East Beach Rd

Lake Crescent Lodge

R

START

P ♿

END

P ♿

North Shore Picnic Area

Lake Crescent

Fairholm Store and Campground

♿ ▲

101

To Forks

0   1   2
Miles

About half of the Spruce Railroad Trail is curvy, narrow, rough, and sometimes rocky. You'll cross rockslide residue and drainage divets, some carrying streams; horses would have a tough time here. The other half of the trail, mostly in the west, is fairly flat and unobstructed. The park suggests wearing long pants to ward off deer ticks; bright-colored clothing will help you spot the critters. If one visits you, dress it in petroleum jelly. They suffocate in five minutes and can be scraped off.

Although you can access the trail from either end, this description begins at its eastern trailhead. From here, the trail heads up into the woods and remains beside the lake, either at water level or on a bank 100 to 200 feet high. A lovely bridge detours around the collapsed 460-foot McFee Tunnel. All that remains is a pile of debris above the west side of the bridge. At 3 miles, look east to see the small Daley-Rankin bore. Observe from outside the tunnels only: The fallen timber and falling rocks here not only are dangerous but also pose a fire hazard to the hillside above.

Though Pacific madrone trees, with their peeling red bark, shade these lower slopes of Pyramid Peak, the southern exposure creates a dry microclimate. In addition to cougars, bear, deer, and raccoons, you might see a golden eagle or a peregrine dropping in from his nesting spot on Pyramid Peak. Look and listen for the pileated woodpecker, the world's largest. Mountain goats, introduced in 1921, remain in the area.

Emerge on Camp David Jr. Road. To extend your adventure, take the road to Fairholm or hike the rugged Pyramid Peak Trail, which climbs 2,400 feet to the peak. Leave from the North Shore picnic area about a mile down the road. Check with the ranger for conditions.

A bridge over a small inlet along the Spruce Railroad Trail.

While you're in the area, you might also visit the Morse Creek to Siebert Creek (Trail 18) and Port Angeles Waterfront (Trail 19) sections of the Olympic Discovery Trail. Or you can continue west for the big ocean tour on the Chehalis Trail Raymond to South Bend Riverfront Trail (Trail 23) and the Astoria Riverwalk (Trail 29). The largest Sitka spruce tree can be found near the Banks-Vernonia State Trail (Trail 30).

The foothills of Mount Rainier and the southern Cascades, green valleys, rivers, creeks, eagles and salmon, small happy towns, and families at play—this is the Foothills Trail. The community created this trail and the community enjoys it. Mount Rainier towers above at such close range that you can almost feel its 14,000 feet of rock, glaciers, and snowfields.

Activities:

Location: Buckley to Orting in Pierce County

Length: There are 9 miles of paved trail in two sections, one 7 miles long, the other 2 miles. The sections aren't contiguous.

Surface: Asphalt with a narrow equestrian path

Wheelchair access: The trail is accessible wherever it's paved.

Difficulty: Easy, except one hill climb

Food: You'll find restaurants and grocery stores in the towns of Buckley and Orting.

Rest rooms: Rest rooms and drinking water are available at the trailheads.

Seasons: The trail can be used year-round.

Access and parking: There are several spots from which to access this trail. To begin at the northwest terminus and enjoy 7 miles of paved trail, use the McMillin Trailhead, found off Route 162. Both Route 410 and Route 165 will take you to this road; to reach it from I–5, take Route 512 and exit at 94th Avenue East. Turn left onto 136th Street East, cross Route 161, turn left onto Military Road East, and then turn right onto 122nd Road. Route 162 is a T at the bottom of the hill. Turn right (south). The trailhead is just south of the trestle over the Puyallup River. It's well signed. You can also continue 2.7 miles along Route 162 to Orting Park and begin there. Beyond that, dirt lots provide trail access near the Carbon River.

You can access the trail's 2-mile Buckley stretch from the town of Buckley. Route 410 will bring you to town; there are two trailheads on this road, one at the armory and one at Ryan Road.

Rentals: No rentals are available near this trail.

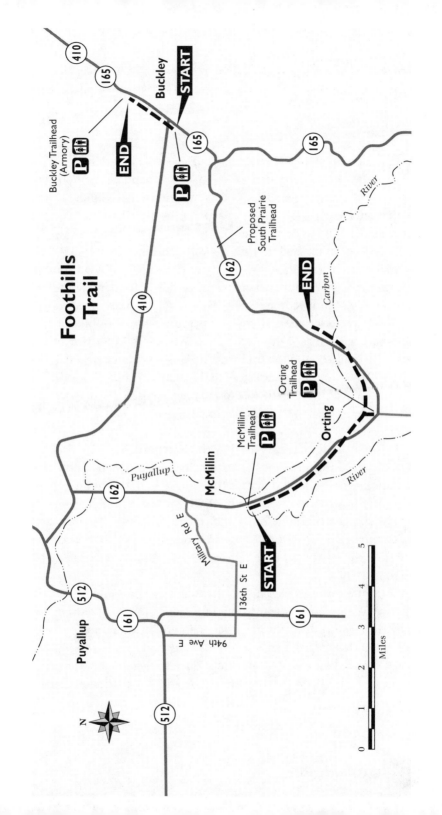

Foothills Trail

Buckley Trailhead
(Armory)

Proposed South Prairie Trailhead

McMillin Trailhead

Orting Trailhead

Orting

Buckley

McMillin

Puyallup

START

END

START

END

410

165

165

165

165

162

162

161

161

410

512

512

512

Military Rd E

136th St E

94th Ave E

Puyallup River

Carbon River

N

Miles

0   1   2   3   4   5

Contact: Foothills Rail-to-Trails Coalition, (253) 841–2570, Bugtrail@aol.com.
Bus routes: Contact Pierce Transit at (253) 581–8000 or www.ptbus.pierce. wa.us.

. . . .

While much of the Foothills Trail's 16-mile length remains undeveloped, you can access a 7-mile asphalt segment that runs through the town of Orting, crossing rivers and wetlands. There's also a stretch of some 1.8 miles of asphalt through Buckley. The trail is not continuous to Buckley or Carbonado.

This description begins at the McMillin Trailhead, although there are many other ways to enjoy the trail. From this trailhead south to Orting, you'll be traveling an open area beside homes and Route 162. The view of Mount Rainier is spectacular. The grades are minimal, but you may notice them if you're a beginner skater or biker. At 2.3 miles the trail turns right and crosses Whitesell Street Northwest. Reach Orting Park and the trailhead at Calistoga Street West 0.4 mile beyond. You'll find a grocery store and restaurants here. To complete the picture of a rural Northwest town, the slogan IN D'BEAN WE TRUST frames the espresso stop. Stop to experience the history and local pride in the park.

This parkland was purchased by the Northern Pacific Railroad in 1887 for $1.00 from the city of Orting. Trains carried passengers to Spokane on one line and across the country on another. Coal and coke were transported from Carbonado, Fairfax, and Wilkeson; timber was shipped from the forestlands by the St. Paul & Tacoma Lumber Company. Burlington Northern took up the tracks starting in 1985, and the city bought the right-of-way in 1994. Trail construction began in 1996.

Continue through the park to the Route 162 crossing, where the highway turns north toward Buckley. Note the 1904 Odd Fellows Hall. Here the trail heads across fields and beside homes, leaving Route 162. It crosses a paved timber bridge at Voights Creek and passes a buffalo farm. Visit Bernie's Place to watch eagles, enjoy a picnic, or fish this pretty spot. In-season salmon angling is popular here.

Mount Rainier provides a stunning backdrop for the Foothills Trail.
(Courtesy Ernest Bay)

The trail returns to the highway and heads uphill to a trestle crossing. A second trestle crosses the Carbon River. Dirt lots sit on either side of the trestle. (You can leave a car here to make this trail a shuttle trip.) The trail crosses a wetlands area on a long paved timber bridge and becomes a narrow dirt path. The trail is impassable at about 3 miles; turn around and return the way you came.

The 1.8-mile segment of paved trail in Buckley runs parallel to Route 410. It passes through the park, ending at the armory north of town.

Future Plans

The South Prairie Trailhead and 4,000 feet of paved trail will be built near the post office in 2001, when the trail is expected to be completed from Orting to South Prairie. The trail will eventually extend from Orting to Buckley and from Cascade Junction to Carbonado and Wilkeson. Another segment will extend to Sumner and Puyallup and into Tacoma. From Sumner, it will connect with the King County Interurban Trail (Trail 5). The trail in Buckley will continue east to Enumclaw and King County. The tremendous efforts of the Foothills Rails-to-Trails Coalition created this trail. Get in touch with the coalition (see "Contact," above) to become part of this continuing effort.

This peaceful trail hides you from a commercial district near I–5, just a few miles from the state capitol in Olympia. It passes beside homes, then farms and ponds, finally reaching the Woodard Bay Conservation Area near Puget Sound. Horses are accommodated with a separate path for most of the way, sometimes through the woods. The sights and sounds of ponds, pastures, forest, birds, ducks, and cows make this a delightful trail, well designed for all users.

Activities:

Location: Olympia, in Thurston County

Length: 5.5 miles

Surface: Asphalt with a dirt horse trail (separated for much of the distance)

Wheelchair access: The entire trail is wheelchair accessible.

Difficulty: Easy

Food: You'll find restaurants on Martin Way at the trail's southern terminus.

Rest rooms: There are rest rooms at the Woodard Bay lot and at midtrail, but no running water.

Seasons: The trail can be used year-round.

Access and parking: You can park your car and access the trail from several cross streets in the area, which have small parking areas. To reach these lots, exit I–5 at Sleater-Kinney Road and head straight (north) to South Bay Road. Turn left and then right onto Shincke Road to a trailhead. Turn left off Shincke at any of the small streets beyond (north) for other trailheads.

There's also a parking lot at the Woodard Bay Conservation Area. To reach this, turn left off Shincke Road at 36th Avenue Northeast, then turn right onto Grays Harbor Road, and right again onto Woodard Bay Road.

To reach the trail's southern terminus (no parking) at Martin Way, turn left onto Martin Way off Sleater-Kinney Road soon after exiting I–5 and look to the right for a bus stop within a few blocks. The trail leaves from the sidewalk here. A final option is to try to get permission to park at a commercial establishment along Martin Way.

Rentals: Olympic Outfitters is at 407 4th Avenue East in Olympia.

Contact: Washington State Department of Natural Resources, (360) 748–2383

Bus routes: None

• •

Although you can access the pleasant Chehalis Western Trail from many points along its way, this description takes you from its southern terminus at Martin Way. The trail begins just off I–5 on a busy street. It's mostly flat with a bit of grade here and there.

Once you depart Martin Way, you'll pass by homes and a little pond. Cross 26th Avenue Northeast at 1.5 miles; the horse trail starts here. You'll travel past horse pastures and wetlands and through evergreens and blackberry vines. Cross South Bay Road at mile 2.5, then Shincke Road soon after. Interpretive and map signs are placed at each intersection. See pictures of locomotives and read the history of timber transport along this route. Logs were hauled to Henderson Inlet by rail and then to the Everett mills by water.

Fields extend far in one direction, and a duck pond straddles the trail. Grab a bench to enjoy the serenity. Find a rest room at 3.25

A dirt equestrian path runs alongside the paved trail used by skaters and other trail users.

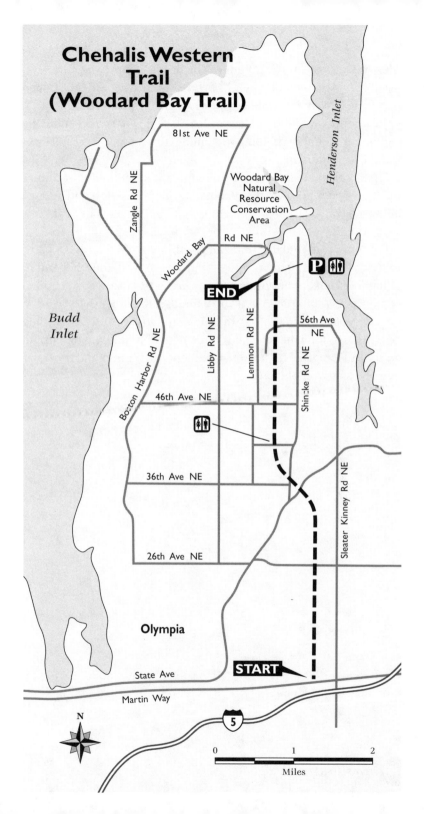

Chehalis Western Trail (Woodard Bay Trail)

81st Ave NE

Zangle Rd NE

Woodard Bay
Natural
Resource
Conservation
Area

Henderson Inlet

Woodard Bay Rd NE

END

P

Budd
Inlet

Boston Harbor Rd NE

Libby Rd NE

Lemmon Rd NE

Shincke Rd NE

56th Ave NE

46th Ave NE

36th Ave NE

Sleater Kinney Rd NE

26th Ave NE

Olympia

State Ave

START

Martin Way

5

N

0   1   2
Miles

miles, just north of 41st Avenue Northeast. After two more street crossings—46th and 56th—you'll arrive at the Woodard Bay Conservation Area. Walk 0.5 mile on the Overlook Trail to Henderson Inlet. Rest at this wooded, waterfront spot, which was once a bustling logging transfer area. If you parked here, drive out to Boston Harbor for another waterfront view.

If you complete the trail round trip, check out the Main Chinese Buffet several miles east on Martin Way. To purchase a gourmet picnic for the trail or indulge at a great salad bar, Top Foods is also east on Martin Way.

For more trail touring, you can continue on the southern part of the Chehalis Trail, which begins approximately 1 mile beyond I-5 at Chambers Lake. The southern section is administered by Thurston County Parks (360-786-5595) and extends 7 miles south to 103rd Avenue. Or you can try the Foothills Trail in Orting (Trail 23), or head to Olympia to tour the lake beside the capitol building. For a unique and soulful experience, head farther south to Tenino and howl with the wolves at Wolf Haven.

South Bend and Raymond, Washington, aren't on the way to anywhere (unless you're heading to Long Beach or Astoria for some oceanfront R&R). You have to *want* to come here. You have to like rural "unyupppified" communities with regional pride, history, and art. You have to appreciate blue herons and outdoor sculpture. A taste for fresh oysters might come in handy, too.

Activities:

Location: between Raymond and South Bend, in Pacific County

Length: 3.5 miles

Surface: Asphalt

Wheelchair access: The trail is not wheelchair accessible.

Difficulty: Easy

Food: You'll find things to eat in both South Bend and Raymond.

Rest rooms: You'll find rest rooms and drinking water at the Raymond Trailhead. Public rest rooms are also located at the South Bend City Park at the southern end of town.

Seasons: The trail can be used year-round, but it's often windy and wet in winter.

Access and parking: The Raymond Trailhead lies in the park at the Willapa Seaport Museum. Turn north from Route 101 on Heath Street (which turns into Alder Street) across from the Raymond Visitors Center. The museum and trailhead are on your left near the end of the road. Take a quick walk down the trail from the road's dead end to see the railroad bridge.

To start in South Bend, turn (north) toward the river on Summit Street just north of town.

Rentals: There are no rentals available along this trail.

Contact: Raymond Chamber of Commerce, (360) 942–5419 (summer only); or Raymond Public Works, (360) 942–3451

Bus routes: None

Explore a pair of rewarding small towns on this trail, the only completed section of the in-progress Chehalis Trail (Raymond to South Bend Riverfront Trail). Your starting point, off-the-beaten-track South Bend, doesn't just claim to be the oyster capital of the world. The county courthouse is also on the National Register of Historic Places, and a bayside sculpture recognizes Joe Krupa, a resident who brought home the prestigious World War II Medal of Honor. The Joe Krupa Wayside Park also offers picnic tables and a portable toilet.

Raymond, on the other hand, boasts a Wildlife-Heritage Sculpture Corridor, funded by the U.S. Coastal Corridor Program to visually enhance Route 101. The community worked together to determine the essence of Raymond. Artists then developed images to portray that essence: Willapa Bay with its nearby hills and the native flora and fauna, the community's history, the logging, fishing, and farming. A steel fabricator produced the 200 designs except for the hand-sculpted three-dimensional works.

You can access the trail from either end, but this description takes you from South Bend northeast into Raymond. From the Krupa Wayside Park, the trail leaves the right-of-way and heads toward the town of Raymond. You'll parallel the highway at close range for a bit, then drop to the water, hills standing across the river. Just beyond, turn left onto the road and right at the stop sign. The trail begins again after a short pass through the Port of Willapa Harbor parking lot. You get a break from the highway before you cross the river on Route 101. The trail then turns left onto Heath Street, taking you to the Raymond Trailhead and the interpretive area near the museum.

Explore Raymond's Third Street to see the old theater and more sculptures. The Raymond Seaport Museum at the trailhead offers more glimpses of local history. When you're ready, turn around and return to South Bend for your reward: oysters at East Point Seafood, located in a cannery on the riverside, south of the trailhead at Summit. Barges bring them in fresh daily. The artistic highlight of this town is the 1911 Pacific County Courthouse, 2 blocks off Route 101 on a hill overlooking the bay and the hills. Walk among the faux marble pillars; look down at the mosaic tile floor and gaze up at the lit art glass dome, 29 feet in diameter. Outside you can picnic by the

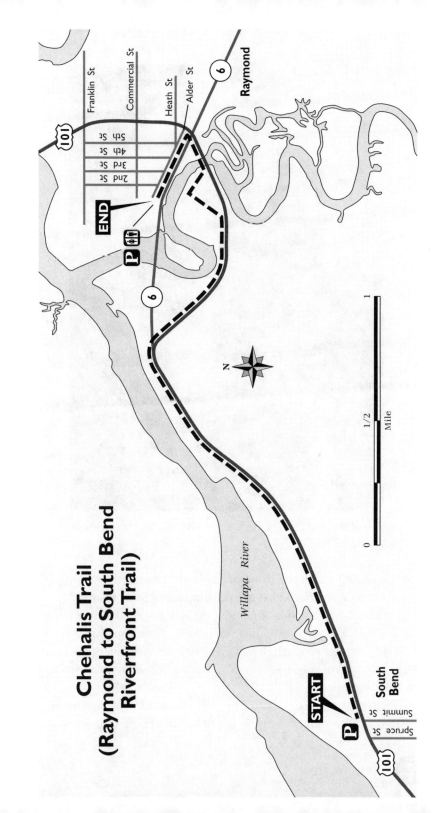

Chehalis Trail
(Raymond to South Bend Riverfront Trail)

Franklin St

Commercial St

Heath St

Alder St

101

6 Raymond

2nd St
3rd St
4th St
5th St

END

P

6

N

Willapa River

START

P

Spruce St

Summit St

South Bend

101

0   1/2   1
Mile

One of the many sculptures along Raymond's Wildlife-Heritage Sculpture Corridor.

duck pond and watch the trout swim about. The Pacific County Historical Society Museum also offers glimpses of local history.

If you're up for a mountain bike ride, Raymond is thirty-five minutes from Montesano and Lake Sylvia State Park; see Trail 24.

The Raymond to South Bend Riverfront Trail will eventually cross Route 101 and follow Route 6 to Chehalis, ultimately connecting to the John Wayne Pioneer Trail.

The redesign of the Third Street business loop of Raymond includes bike lanes all the way to Route 105 along the ocean.

24 Lake Sylvia State Park

Lake Sylvia State Park has something for everyone: logging history and operations, a dam, a thirty-acre lake, camping, picnicking, and any number of great trails to explore. Two of these trails—the Sylvia Creek Forestry Trail and the Two Mile Trail—are featured here. Both are secluded in a forest of western hemlock and Douglas fir, some of which is part of a working tree farm. Though the trails are managed by two different agencies and for different purposes, they are contiguous with each other and offer a similar forest experience and a great workout.

Activities:

Location: Grace Harbor County

Length: 4.8 miles total. The Sylvia Creek Forestry Trail is 2.8 miles long; the Two Mile Trail is 2 miles.

Surface: Dirt and gravel, the trail can be very muddy.

Wheelchair access: The trails are not wheelchair accessible, but access is available at the park and lakeside.

Difficulty: The Two Mile Trail is easy along its 0.75-mile flat stretch, difficult along the 1.25-mile hiking trail. The Sylvia Creek Forestry Trail is difficult.

Food: There are vending machines in the park; you'll also find restaurants and groceries in Montesano.

Rest rooms: The park features rest rooms and drinking water.

Seasons: The trails are open year-round, though they can be wet in fall and winter.

Access and parking: To reach Lake Sylvia State Park, take exit 104 off I–5 onto Route 101 west toward Aberdeen. Where Route 101 exits, stay on Route 8. Continue to Route 107, signed MONTESANO, LAKE SYLVIA STATE PARK. Turn right into town. Follow signs to the park: Drive through the stoplight, turn left at the stop sign (East Spruce Avenue), then turn right onto North Third Street. You'll arrive at the Lake Sylvia parking area 1.5 miles from Route 8.

Rentals: No rentals are available along the trail.

Contact:
- City of Montesano, (360) 249–3021
- Lake Sylvia State Park, (360) 249–3621
- Washington State Parks, (800) 233–0321, www.parks.wa.gov/lksylvia.htm

Bus routes: None

• •

Lake Sylvia State Park has a lot to explore. The park's thirty-acre lake contains native bass and stocked trout. Coho salmon and trout live in Sylvia Creek; beavers build dams along its banks, while otters play in the water. Bears and birds love the sweet grasses, berries, and bushes in the open replanted areas of the forestry trail. A play area, picnic sites, and a boat launch combine with interpretive trails to offer a full day of recreation; a campground lets you extend your visit.

History is highlighted throughout the park as well. The original dam was built in 1868 to power the first sawmill in Grays Harbor County. The backwater pond was used for log flotation. You can see the suprastructure when the lake is lowered. The present dam was built in the 1920s to provide Montesano with power. The land became a state park in 1936.

A tree-tunnel on the Sylvia Creek Forestry Trail.

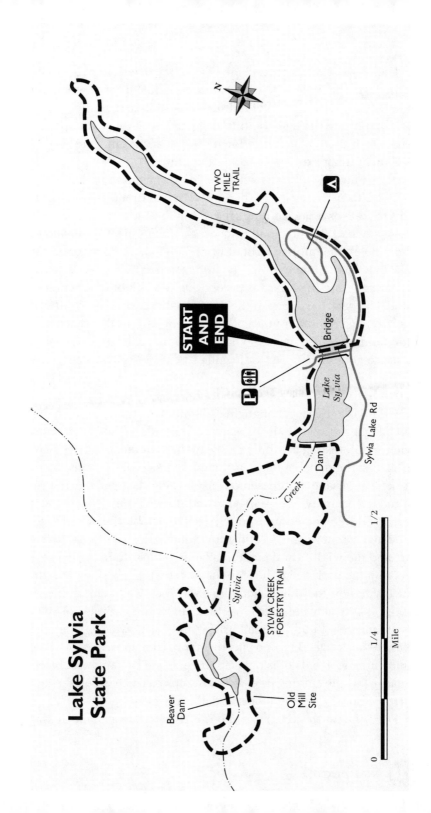

Lake Sylvia State Park

TWO MILE TRAIL

START AND END

Bridge

Lake Sylvia

P

Sylvia Lake Rd

Creek

Dam

Sylvia

SYLVIA CREEK FORESTRY TRAIL

Beaver Dam

Old Mill Site

N

0   1/4   1/2
Mile

Look for a carved 4-foot sphere of wood used for leisure log rolling in the lake, the underwater log dam, remnants of the sawmill, and old trestles. These 3 miles of railroad were built to haul timber from the pond to the Chehalis County Logging and Timber Company in 1905. Oxen then hauled it to town. The hearty oxen were the sole method of timber transport before the railroad.

A vast network of trails will take you through the park. This description focuses on two of them: The Sylvia Creek Forestry Trail, built in 1991, is a rugged interpretive trail beside Sylvia Creek with short, steep hills, and small bridges; the Two Mile Trail heads out 0.75 mile on the railroad right-of-way, then loops 1.25 miles around Lake Sylvia on a hiking trail. The undeveloped right-of-way continues straight into the forest as part of the network of mountain bike trails. The park has a map of the entire trail network; many offer especially desirable mountain biking. (They are, in fact, used for a mountain bike race each September.) Some trails are also logging roads, so you may encounter logging trucks.

Sylvia Creek Forestry Trail (SCFT)

The SCFT is a rugged, challenging 2.8-mile-long trail. For the mountain biker, it's strewn with obstacles and hazards; for the hiker, it provides an interesting and hilly pathway through the forest. The land up against the park boundaries, including this trail, is owned by the city of Montesano and leased out for logging. Logging created this railroad bed ninety-five years ago, and it's still going strong today. The city developed an interpretive trail to exhibit this working forest. The clear-cuts, the second-growth forest, the old Chehalis mill site, and the wildlife and plant habitat are all part of this display.

From the parking lot, head to the dam on the lakeside path. The SCFT starts on the uphill side of a short rock wall behind the rest rooms. Bikers may prefer to cross the dam to the south side of Sylvia Creek and ride to the railroad bridge and back, avoiding the more difficult north side. If you do bike the north side, stop or slow at every blind curve to avoid collisions with hikers, and be cautious of steep banks below the curving trail, wooden steps placed in steep sections, narrow bridges, and mudholes. Ride in control.

From the north side, the trail heads downhill to a creek crossing at 0.65 mile and up a steep hill. The second creek crossing is on a short, narrow bridge. Steep steps follow; a short downhill leads to a burned-out tree that creates an archway on the trail at mile 1.0. Shortly after that, a gaping hole all but eliminates the trail. The riverbank is steep here. Be sure, if you're on a bike, that your brakes and rims aren't too muddy to keep you on the trail. At mile 1.15, the clear-cut opens the wooded trail up to sunshine. Steps take you downhill to the creek crossing at 1.4 miles.

The trail levels out to rolling terrain for a while. The flat area to your right is the site of the sawmill that operated in the late 1800s. The trestle pilings can be seen on your left. At 1.83 miles, steps follow a curve that takes you downhill to a narrow bridge and onto a second bridge almost concealed by a curve in the trail. Walk up a long hill on steps. Wind around in the deep evergreen forest high on the banks of Sylvia Creek until you reach a dramatic view of the drop below the dam. Watch the edge here. Cross the dam to return to the park.

Two Mile Trail

The Two Mile Trail begins adjacent to the small parking area near the bridge that crosses the lake. It runs flat along the lake, a bench

Bridge across Lake Sylvia.

Stream crossing on the Sylvia Creek Forestry Trail.

placed here and there. At the gate at 0.75 mile, climb up to a bridge (over the middle fork of Sylvia Creek) and turn right to continue the Two Mile Trail around the lake. The actual right-of-way, called C-line Road, goes straight ahead past another gate. It continues flat for 2 miles, then heads uphill. A steeper logging road heads off to the right. Be sure to take a bike map if you'd like to venture off to the many trails outside the park boundaries. The Two Mile Trail loop climbs up steps and descends to narrow bridges, only to climb again to a bank high above the lake. The trail is narrow and pretty. Use the interpretive guide to follow the numbered posts to identify wildflowers, trees, and logging features. The trail drops you off at the campground, and from there the road returns you to your starting point.

On your way out of Montesano, be sure visit the historic county building on Broadway, 1 block downhill from Spruce. Other nearby rail-trails include the Chehalis Trail (Trail 23), thirty-five minutes from Montesano, and the Chehalis Western Trail (Trail 22), north of Olympia off I–5.

Grays Harbor County has quite a number of abandoned railbeds. Meetings are in progress to work toward linking them together as trails.

25 John Wayne Pioneer Trail (West)

The John Wayne Pioneer Trail crosses most of Washington State. The developed portion lies within the Iron Horse State Park. It parallels I–90 from Cedar Falls, near North Bend, to Kittitas, then drops south through army land to end on the edge of the magnificent Columbia River.

The trail passes through various climatic zones. West of the Cascades are the wet and green Cascade foothills. East of the mountains you'll find glacial valleys with pine and fir trees and ranchland. As you continue east, the landscape changes to sagebrush desert, arid scrublands, and the irrigated farmlands of the Columbia Basin. East of Thorp the trail is unshaded and dry, hot in summer and cold in winter. Bear, bobcats, cougars, rattlesnakes, eagles, ospreys, rodents, rabbits, and butterflies inhabit different parts of the trail.

Activities.

Location: Cedar Falls to the Columbia River

Length: 113 miles

Surface: Compacted ballast, gravel, and sand; the trail is 16 to 20 feet wide. The section from Cedar Falls to Easton has the most compacted surface.

Wheelchair access: This trail is not wheelchair accessible.

Difficulty: Easy to moderate, with some sandy and rocky surfaces. There's a constant 1.75 percent grade uphill from Cedar Falls to Hyak.

Food: You can find things to eat in Ellensburg, Easton, and Kittitas, and at the intersection with Thorp Prairie Highway. In winter try the Hyak Ski Lodge.

Rest rooms: You'll find rest rooms at all trailheads except Easton, Ellensburg, and Kittitas; they're also available along the trail between Cedar Falls and Hyak. Water is available at most trailheads.

Camping: You'll find campgrounds at Lake Kachess, Lake Easton State Park, the Wanapum Recreation Area, the Army East Trailhead, and Kittitas County Fairgrounds.

Seasons: The trail can be used year-round, although the Snoqualmie Tunnel is closed November 1 through April 30. Cross-country skiing or snowshoeing is fun here between December and March; the trail is groomed on weekends from Hyak to Crystal Springs or Lake Easton State Park.

Access and parking: You'll need a special Sno-Park permit to park at Hyak, Easton, or Lake Easton State Park in winter. Contact local outdoor stores or the U.S. Forest Service office adjacent to the Summit Ski Area at exit 52.

- *Cedar Falls* (exit 32): Take Cedar Falls Road off I–90 and drive 3 miles south to the Rattlesnake Lake parking lot. Park and continue up the road 0.5 mile to the trailhead on your left.
- *Twin Falls* (exit 38): If you're driving east on I–90, turn right at the end of the exit and park in the lot marked TWIN FALLS NATURAL AREA. If you're heading westbound, take a left off the exit ramp, drive 2 miles, and park in the second lot on your left.
- *Hyak* (exit 54): At the end of the ramp, make a soft left onto the frontage road. Turn right at the sign that reads IRON HORSE STATE PARK to enter the Lake Keechelus parking lot. A Sno-Park permit is required in winter.
- *Lake Easton State Park* (exit 70): To head west on the trail, get to the frontage road south of I–90 and drive east to the park entrance. Pass the ranger booth and take the first right. Park in the day-use area straight ahead. To reach the trail, turn left out of the lot, pass through a closed gate, turn left at the dead end onto a dirt road, and finally turn right onto the trail. A Sno-Park permit is required in winter.
- *Easton* (exit 71): To head east on the trail, follow the signs from the exit to Easton. Cross the railroad tracks and turn left at the trail sign. A Sno-Park permit is required in winter.
- *South Cle Elum (*exit 84): Follow the signs to South Cle Elum, turning left on the main drag and left again at the tourist office on your left and the flagged park on your right. Follow signs to Iron Horse State Park.
- *Thorp* (exit 101): Head 0.25 mile north on Thorp Highway. Turn left onto Thorp Depot Road and drive another 0.25 mile to the trail crossing and the trailhead beyond.
- *Ellensburg West* (exit 106): To head west on the trail, follow signs to Central Washington University north of I–90. The trailhead is on Water Street near 14th Avenue. Note that neither Ellensburg trailhead has any facilities, but there are plenty of facilities between the two.
- *Ellensburg East* (exit 109): Turn north onto Main Street. At 2 miles, turn right on Eighth Avenue. Drive 0.8 mile more, then look for the KITTITAS COUNTY FAIRGROUNDS sign on your right. Eighth becomes 10th. You'll see a Starbucks on your left and a grocery and burger place on your right. Park in the college lot behind Starbucks ($1.00 during the week). Take the first right east of the fairgrounds sign (Alder Street). Alder dead-ends at the rodeo entrance. The trail restarts here between a trailer park and the rodeo entrance, on an unmarked dirt mound. Head uphill to the east. Signage begins only after you pass through the gate at the top of the hill. Note that neither Ellensburg trailhead has any facilities, but there are plenty of facilities between the two.

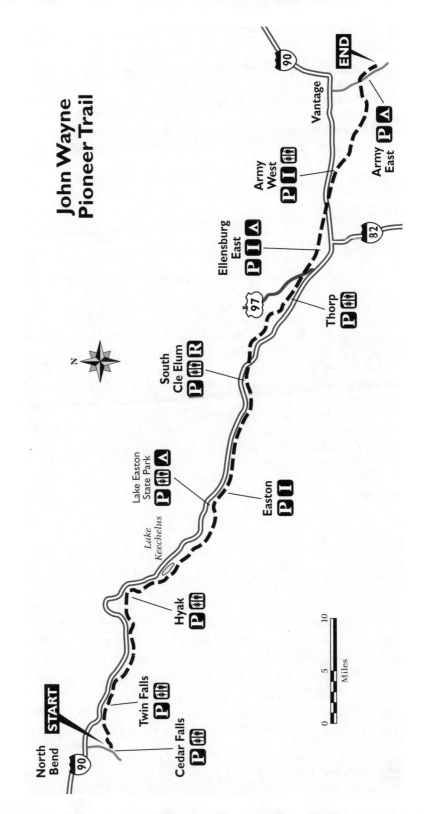

John Wayne
Pioneer Trail

- *Kittitas* (exit 115): Head north from the freeway. Turn left onto Railroad Avenue and park near the depot or in town.
- *Army West* (exit 115): Continue north on Main Street past the Kittitas Trailhead to First Street and turn right. First becomes Parke Creek Road and parallels the trail for 2.5 miles. Turn right onto Prater Road to cross I–90, then left onto Boyleston and right at the T-intersection with Stevens Road. The trailhead is on your left.
- *Army East* (exit 136): From the freeway, travel south on Huntzinger Road past the Wanapum Recreation Area. Cross the trail and turn right onto the Yakima Training Center access road. You'll find the trailhead in 2 miles.

Rentals: You can rent mountain bikes at Bike and Hike in Cle Elum, (509) 674–4567.

Contact:
- For trail information, contact the Washington State Parks hotline at (800) 233–0321 or visit www.parks.wa.gov.
- Lake Easton State Park can be reached at (509) 656–2586.
- The Wanapum Recreation Area's phone number is (509) 856–2700.
- For information on camping, call Washington State Parks (May 15 through September 15) at (800) 452–5687. The number for the hearing impaired is (800) 858–9659.
- For information on Kittitas County Fairgrounds camping, call (509) 962–7639.
- The number for tourism information in Ellensburg is (509) 925–3137. For North Bend call the East King County Visitors Bureau at (425) 455–1926; www.eastkingcounty.org.
- To learn about the history of the Milwaukee Road Railroad, visit www.mrha.com.

Bus routes: None

• •

I ron Horse State Park includes 113 miles of rail-trail and more than 1,600 acres of adjacent land. The trail is isolated much of the way. There are no services on the trail east of Kittitas. There is presently no bicycle or pedestrian or equestrian crossing to the town of Beverly, where the eastern section of trail begins, across the river.

Snow cover for cross-country skiing and snowshoeing usually lasts from December through March and is most reliable from Hyak to Crystal Springs or Easton. Ski tracks are groomed in winter. Some areas east of the mountains have intermittent snow cover.

In 1917 the Milwaukee Road (of the Chicago, Milwaukee, St. Paul & Pacific Railroad) became the first electrified transcontinental railroad and the nation's longest electrified train. This not only helped clear smoke from the tunnels, but also eliminated the time-consuming job of setting the brakes on mountain switchbacks. The electric railway was so well designed that it operated from 1917 into the 1970s with few problems. Trains braking while heading down-hill regenerated power back into the overhead catenary wires to power the uphill trains. The line opened for freight in 1909, and the Olympian-Hiawatha passenger train made its debut in 1911. The last Milwaukee train passed over the Cascades in 1980. The state opened the first segment of the rail-trail in 1984 and added the trestle at Hall Creek in 1999. Only two trestles remain to be decked, east of Thorp.

Hyak to Cedar Falls, 22.5 miles

From Snoqualmie Pass to the lowland town of North Bend, this portion of the John Wayne Trail guides you through 2.25 miles of tunnel, above the Snoqualmie River Valley on high trestles, and below mountain peaks. Pass beside creeks and waterfalls, under huge fir trees, and beside a large blue lake bounded by the vertical walls of Mount Si. It's quite a treat to be perched above the valley and dwarfed below the mountain peaks, watching the moving picture of the Cascade Mountains and valleys below you.

The author cross-country skiing near the Lake Keechelus Sno-Park at Hyak.

Although you can travel either way on the trail, this segment from Hyak to Cedar Falls is described going east to west. The constant 1.75 percent grade of 2,500 vertical feet makes this section an easier downhill ride going west for cyclists. Plus many people visit the trail just to see the tunnel at the east end of this segment.

You can park cars at both trailheads or ride up I–90 and down the trail. To reach the western trailhead, see "Access and parking," above. Cedar Falls can also serve as the trailhead for a multiday trip across the state via bicycle, horse, ski, or foot. The Snoqualmie Valley Trail extension reaches Rattlesnake Lake for those connecting from other trails.

Descending this section of the old Milwaukee Railroad is as sad as it is scenic. Local history describes ski instructors boarding the Seattle train on Friday night for a weekend of work and play. They hopped off the train and trudged through the snow to their bunkhouse. These were the days of the tow rope and the Milwaukee ski jump. A few old boards remain on the hillside. Modern skiers couldn't be convinced to ride the rails; they wanted the convenience and flexibility of their cars.

Still, the abandonment of this railroad has given way to new adventures, new ways to raise our spirits and our heart rates. The 22.5-mile segment is the most heavily used. The rail station at Hyak now houses individual bathrooms, large enough for a small party—a great amenity for cold skiers. The Hyak ski area (called Summit East) lies directly uphill. The Summit Cross Country Ski Trail runs just above the rail-trail and encircles Mount Catherine for a hillier, groomed ski tour.

From the Lake Keechelus parking lot, join the trail westbound. You'll shortly enter the east portal of the 2.25-mile Snoqualmie Tunnel. Bring a light and a jacket: The ceiling drips water in several spots, and it's cold and dark. It's also spooky and a lot of fun. You'll be able to see the beams of light from oncoming walkers, horses, and cyclists. A miniature archway of light shines from the west end of the tunnel. The archway grows slowly until you exit under its 30-foot ceiling. You'll emerge on the edge of a river gully with Outlook Mountain in your face. Look back to see the engraved sign that reads SNOQUALMIE TUNNEL. Cyclists and walkers around you are removing

Supports for the electric wires of the old Milwaukee Road still stand at Hansen Creek Trestle.

their long sleeves and replacing their sunglasses. It's time to head down the trail and enjoy the view and the downhill grade. The trail is mostly open with great mountain views.

Pass beside a wooden snowshed at mile 5.5 before reaching the curving trestle at Hansen Creek at mile 8.5. Beware of missing cables on the bridge sides. You can see the overhead supports for the electric lines. A creek falls steeply down the center of a mountain cirque. It drops below the trestle and draws your eyes to the valley. The gravel on the new trestles is bigger and harder to ride on a bike: Stroll across and enjoy the scenery.

The Snoqualmie Tunnel at Hyak.

You'll cross creeks and valley views, seeing waterfalls against the steep hillsides. McClellan Butte comes into sight straight ahead, and you enter a lowland forest. The last few miles are rockier and steeper. Mount Si makes a pretty picture when it comes into view.

At mile 16, cross the modern trestle at Hall Creek. A collapsed link was replaced in spring 1999, so the trail is now passable without your having to leave the railroad grade. Just beyond, you'll pass a busy stream of rock jocks climbing Deception Crags.

A road cuts down to Olallie State Park from here. The next hiking trail that drops off to the right takes you to the 75-foot free-span wooden bridge over waterfalls in Twin Falls State Park.

At the gated end of the trail, turn right on the road to reach Rattlesnake Lake or to descend to North Bend on the Snoqualmie Valley Trail Extension. Catch the trail across the street from the parking lot. (See Trail 10.) Don't forget to enjoy a pastry at George's Bakery on North Bend Way.

Hyak to Easton, 18 miles

Heading east from the Snoqualmie Tunnel or the Hyak, enjoy 18 miles of gentle downhill and flat grade as you drop from 2,500 feet to 2,176 feet. The trail follows the edge of Lake Keechelus until you reach The Keechelus Dam. You will find yourself on a corridor bounded by bright green foliage, rock faces, and the deep blue Lake Keechelus, which is interrupted by the occasional tiny island. The gentle sound of water teasing the banks of the lake makes this a great place to stop. Little white wildflowers and tiny patches of lavender blossoms color the trail in summer while frosted peaks and the icy lake change the landscape in winter.

Cross Meadows Creek and the road to Lost Lake at mile 6. Once past the lake, the conical, ivory heads of Bear Grass cluster here and there. The trail parallels the dirt Stampede Pass Road until crossing it at 7.5 miles. At mile 10, pass through the short, dark, and rocky Whittier Tunnel. Then head left at the fork. Between miles 14 and 15 you will pass over creeks and high above the Yakima River on the secluded, wooded trail. Detour left onto a dirt path at the sign to Easton and the Iron Horse Trail. The dirt road angles right onto a paved road beside Lake Easton. (From the gate here, it will be another 2.3 miles along the road until you reach the Easton trailhead.) At the first intersection, you will find rest rooms, water, a beach, and picnic tables to the right. Turn left to continue and left again to reach the park exit. Turn right (east) to exit Lake Easton Park onto the frontage road. Arrive in the tiny town of Easton on Railroad Street. Pass CB's general store with snacks and sandwiches. Turn right at the post office and left at the IRON HORSE STATE PARK sign. A dirt road takes you to the park and the trailhead, where you'll find picnic tables, a hitching post, rest rooms, and water. A kiosk provides trail information.

Easton to Cle Elum, 11.5 miles

As you depart from the downtown Easton Trailhead, you'll enjoy a slight downhill grade and a good surface. The trail runs close to I–90 in places, though it's buffered by pine and fir trees. The mountains shrink into rounded hills; an occasional ranch appears on the landscape. Cross Golf Course Road and an I–90 interchange at 6 miles and twin trestles just beyond. Listen for the clicking of grasshoppers on the trail. At mile 9.5, the Yakima River rushes under the trail and leaves just as quickly. Violet and yellow wildflowers accompany the wild, white daisies.

Marshes and creek crossings give the trail some interest as you approach the old Cle Elum railroad station and substation. This is one of two remaining depots; the second still stands in Kittitas. As you pass the depot, the substation, and a trail kiosk, you can exit at Main Street and lounge in a park found 1 block away. Continue straight on Main to head into South Cle Elum for food, lodging, and espresso.

Cle Elum was a lively town in railroading days—a crew-change town. When the train was electrified, the crew bunkhouse was moved to its present location on Sixth Street a few blocks east of the depot. It's now the Iron Horse B&B. If you call ahead to book a room or a caboose, you can enjoy the warmth of this establishment and the wealth of railroad history the proprietors have to share.

Trestle over Yakima River west of Cle Elum.

Active tracks and trail parallel the river between Cle Elum and Thorp.

Cle Elum to Thorp, 18.6 miles

The trail is a bit rougher as you leave Cle Elum, with more loose gravel. Pass under I-90 at mile 3.16, leaving it south of the trail. The Yakima River (and Route 10) appears to your left at mile 5; look for rafters and anglers in the fast waters below the trail. The green of the foliage and the pine trees create a pleasant pathway, and the slight downhill grade eases your journey.

As you enter the Upper Yakima River Canyon, the river widens, trees become sparse, and hills are round and brown. Tall walls of basalt appear. The only shade you'll find is inside Tunnels 46 and 47. You'll be in the dark for a few seconds on a bike—a bit longer on foot—in the western tunnel. The eastern tunnel is short. Grasshoppers conduct their loud symphony of clicking. Tiny birds whisk about the trees, and striking black-and-yellow monarch butterflies disperse when you hit the wet potholes from which they drink. They'll escort you for a bit, then find another watering spot. Perhaps a muskrat will scurry by or a rabbit will bounce down the trail.

As the last cliffs disappear, you emerge into an expanse of ranchland bordered by foothills in the distance. Cows stare from behind barbed wire. Pass through two gates. Be sure to resecure them behind you after you pass through.

Arrive at the Thorp Trailhead at mile 18.6. The kiosk reads, "Prairie grasslands dominate the landscape. Looking eastward it's all you can see for miles. Grasslands blend into sage-covered hills and the fertile farmland of the Columbia River basin." You have arrived at another transition zone.

You may want to make a stop at the Fruit and Antique Mall just across Thorp Prairie Highway and to your right, near the I–90 exit ramp. Piles of fresh fruit, jams, ice cream, beverages, and espresso await. Sample the feta and pink peppercorn dip or artichoke dip and view the antique carriages.

Thorp to Ellensburg East, 8.4 miles

Hop back on the trail to Ellensburg—or take a 9-mile detour to avoid two undecked trestles with some gaps between the ties and some rotten wood. To detour, head south on Thorp Prairie Highway across I–90. The highway parallels the interstate and crosses back over it at the West Ellensburg interchange. Turn left at the four-way stop onto Route 97 northbound. You'll pass a substation before you see the trail on your right. The trestles will be decked in late 2001 to mid-2002.

If you stay on the trail, leave the noise of I–90 behind and enjoy the flat, open farmland and the occasional shade of a crab apple tree. Passage around several gates is narrow and sloping—they're tough to get around on a bike or a horse. You'll reach the first of two undecked trestles at mile 2.2. They cross Route 10 and the active railroad tracks. Cross carefully: Aside from gaps, the trestles have deep gravel. At 3 miles, use caution crossing Route 97.

Reach the Ellensburg West Trailhead at Water Street at 6.8 miles. A kiosk displays the route you might want to use to take a 1.6-mile detour through town. Turn right on Water Street and left on 14th Avenue, which becomes Dean Nicholson Way as you pass through the college. Turn right at the T-intersection, Alder Street. Alder dead-ends at the Kittitas Fairgrounds rodeo entrance after you cross 10th Avenue. The trail restarts here beside a trailer park, on an unmarked dirt mound. Head uphill to the gate. Signage begins only after you pass through the gate. Neither Ellensburg Trailhead has any facilities, but there are plenty of facilities between the two. From the corner of Alder and 10th, you'll see a Starbucks to your right, U-Tote-Em Burgers just beyond (at Poplar), and a grocery store across the street. Cruise to the historic district and enjoy gourmet food at the Valley Café on Third Street off Main.

Ellensburg East to Army East, 31.5 miles

From the fairgrounds, head through farm country on flat, open trail. If you like, take a side trip to view the 1875 log cabin and homestead of the Olmsteads at Olmstead Place State Park. At mile 6 and 1,674 feet, pull into Kittitas at the second of the two remaining depots. Built in 1909, it's listed on the National Register of Historic Places. The town is smaller than it was in 1884, when it was built in a failed attempt to lure the Northern Pacific Railway. Twenty-four years later the Milwaukee Road built a right-of-way through town to transport the area's grains, fruits, vegetables, and livestock. The railroad came in 1908 and gave the town a post office, as it did in Cle Elum. Once the arid lowlands were irrigated, the fertile soil could produce enough produce to support residents. Check the kiosk to learn how long it took the Olympian-Hiawatha to reach Seattle from Chicago in 1945 on the Milwaukee Road.

There are two taverns, a cafe, and a grocery near the trail. Just across the street from the trailhead is the Fairlane Café and Espres-

Washboard descent through rock cut near Army East. (Courtesy Richard Smith)

so. Open seven days a week, this spot provides a feast for the eyes and treats for the palate. The proprietor of the car shop on the property builds hot rods and has decorated the place in pure 1950s car fashion. Grab some German peppernut cookie bits and enjoy a Kona Mocha with your lunch. Say hi to Debbie. This is your last stop in civilization, and your last predictable water until the Army East Trailhead in 26.6 miles.

Back on the trail, at 8.6 miles, follow the sign to detour right on Prater Street to cross over I–90, then take an immediate left onto

Boylston. Pass some cattle and climb until mile 12, where you'll cross under the trestle responsible for the detour. Turn right at the T-intersection just beyond. Find the Army West Trailhead on your left, complete with rest rooms, water, an informational kiosk, and parking. Pump to start the water flowing.

The trail continues uphill to your right. Follow the sign through the gate at mile 12.75 and complete your entry permit. The next 22 miles are on sandy, rocky, unshaded, desert army property. You will get sucked into the soft surface for the first 4 miles. At mile 16.6, rejoice at the entry to the Boylston Tunnel. It's cool, shaded, and dark for a few seconds. Best of all, the surface improves, and you head downhill for much of the next 18 miles. Passages through the rock cuts are littered with rocks. The remainder of the surface is a bit rough and the grade is slight, but it's a great improvement over the sand.

Drink, drink, and drink again and slather the sunscreen. There's no exit from this area if you become dehydrated, overheated, or worn. At about mile 30, expect a mirage: a dirt road leading to rest rooms, water, and a horse trough. Head left. Check the instructions

Final approach to the Columbia River. (Courtesy Richard Smith)

for turning on the water. This would be a good time to engage your friends in a water fight, particularly if you've chosen a 100-degree day to traverse the desert. You'll find the Army East Trailhead a mile beyond, with parking and camping.

Continue straight on the trail. Enjoy views of the Columbia River and the old trestle in the distance. You can approach the trestle on the trail, but fences prevent access. Turn left at the gate at Huntzinger Road (paved) 2 miles beyond Army East, then turn left to reach the Wanapum Recreation Area, about 4 hilly miles down the road. Here you can camp, find all the amenities, cool off in the Columbia River, and congratulate yourself. The small town of Vantage, I–90, and the bridge across the river are 3 uphill miles ahead. The Gingko Petrified Forest is 1 mile north of Vantage. From here, grab a Greyhound bus or a motel room. Masochists may continue on the John Wayne Pioneer Trail on the east side of the Columbia. (See "More Rail Trails" for information on this eastern segment.)

The Cowiche Canyon Trail takes you through both geological and railroading history. Slicing through a canyon and crossing the creek repeatedly, this rail-trail makes for a tour that's both dramatic and peaceful. You'll have many opportunities to observe plant and animal life.

Activities:

Location: Yakima, Yakima County

Length: 2.9 miles

Surface: Large gravel and dirt

Wheelchair access: The trail is not wheelchair accessible.

Difficulty: Easy

Food: No food is available along this trail.

Rest rooms: You'll find rest rooms at the Weikel Road Trailhead.

Seasons: The trail can be used year-round.

Access and parking: To reach the western trailhead from Yakima, exit Route 12 on North 40th Avenue. Head south to Summitview Avenue. Turn right and drive 7 miles west to Weikel Road. Turn right, drive 0.25 mile, then turn right into the parking area. Continue along the road to the historical kiosk at the trailhead.

Rentals: Try Sagebrush Cycles at 5110 Tieton Drive in Yakima, (509) 972–1330, users.ewa.net/sagecycle/; or Valley Cycling at 1802 West Nob Hill Boulevard in Yakima, (509) 453–6699, www.valleycycleandfitness.com.

Contact: The Cowiche Canyon Conservancy is a nonprofit organization dedicated to protecting the canyon as a natural resource area, and ensuring its recreational use and enjoyment. Call (509) 577–9585 or write P.O. Box 877, Yakima, WA 98907.

Bus routes: None

. . . .

Cowiche Canyon is the result of geological activity that took place millions of years ago. From Pullman, lava flowed to form the Cowiche Canyon floor and the south wall 17.5 million years ago.

This 6,000-foot-thick layer, called the Columbia River Basalts, covered eastern Washington. Then, one million years ago, Tieton Andesite flowed from the west to create the north wall.

In 1913 the North Yakima & Valley Railroad line of the Northern Pacific was built through the canyon to haul apples to Yakima from the productive orchards in Cowiche and Tieton. Workers blasted through vertical basalt cliffs to create the line, which crosses the Cowiche River eleven times. The constant curve of the canyon frames each rock formation ahead and paints a picture of the trains rumbling down the rails.

From the kiosk at the trailhead, travel a slight grade downhill to the first of nine bridges. Portions of the trail contain heavy gravel, making it tough going even for mountain bikes. Beware of a large step up to some of the bridges in addition to the absence of railings. Bikers should dismount if in question. Though sightings are rare, rattlesnakes may be present.

The contrast between the lush riparian vegetation along Cowiche Creek and the browns and yellows of the shrub-steppe on the hillside can only be witnessed in spring. The hot, dry summer months and cold winters put plant life to sleep.

People and pets alike enjoy walking the Cowiche Canyon Trail.

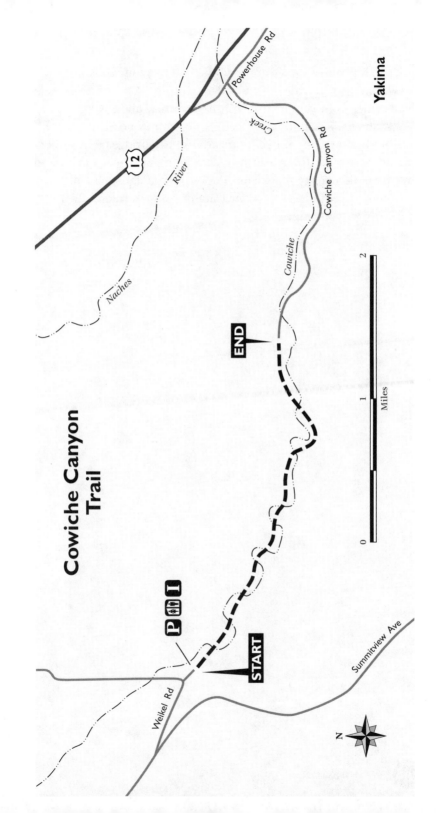

Cowiche Canyon Trail

Yakima

Naches River

I2

Powerhouse Rd

Creek

Cowiche Canyon Rd

Cowiche

END

START

P

Weikel Rd

Summitview Ave

N

0   1   2
Miles

The creek crossings give life to the still canyon. Look and listen for wildlife as you travel from bridge to bridge. The western meadowlark sings from March through June. Marmots and coyotes, canyon wrens, chickadees, and magpies may be seen or heard.

After bridge 8, the trail detours around two bridges that were destroyed during conflicts over trail development. Here you'll be following an old county road. This a poison ivy neighborhood.

When you emerge at Cowiche Canyon Road, turn around and return the way you came.

27 Lower Yakima Valley Pathway

Wineries, sunshine, fresh fruit, and more wineries! This traverse of the world-renowned Yakima Valley wine country will take you past any number of gourmet delights—fine dining, farm stands, candy shops, and, of course, the area's many award-winning wine makers—all in a dusty, unshaded, desert environment.

Activities:

Location: The Yakima Valley towns of Sunnyside, Grandview, and Prosser, in Benton and Yakima Counties

Length: 14.5 miles

Surface: Asphalt, with occasional spots of dirt and gravel

Wheelchair access: The trail is wheelchair accessible in areas, but note rough spots mentioned below.

Difficulty: Easy—though it's moderate for skaters. The trail is narrow (8 to 8.5 feet) and has a bit of grade here and there, along with some rough pavement (noticeable for skaters). It runs on the roadside for 1.5 miles. The Grandview parking area toward Prosser is smoothest for skating.

Food: There are grocery stores, fruit vendors, fast food, restaurants, and wineries along the way.

Rest rooms: There are facilities 3.5 miles east of the western trailhead, and there's water at the East Grandview Trailhead.

Seasons: The trail can be used year-round, though it may be snowy or cold in winter.

Access and parking: Take I–82 from Yakima or from the Tri-Cities of Pasco, Richland, and Kennewick to the exits for Sunnyside (exit 58), Grandview (exit 73), or Prosser (exit 82). The trail parallels Route 12.

Parking areas are located in Sunnyside at North 16th Street, just west of an underpass at the western edge of Grandview, and east of the Grandview commercial district (where the trail restarts on the north side of Route 12). You can also park on the street at the Yakima River crossing in Prosser.

Rentals: No rentals are available along this trail.

Contacts:
- Yakima Valley Tourism, (800) 221–0751
- Yakima Valley Wine Country, (509) 575–3010 (seasonal events)

- Yakima Valley Wine Growers Association, (800) 258–7270
- Washington Wine Commission, www.washingtonwine.org/tripp/yakmap.asp

Bus routes: None

- -

The Lower Yakima Valley Pathway spans three desert towns between Yakima and the Tri-Cities. The desert clime is dry: hot in summer, cold in winter. It's also just right for producing the fine wines of Washington State. Vintners note its location on the forty-sixth parallel—the same as Burgundy and Bordeaux, the great wine-producing regions of France. The soil is twice as productive as most due to nutrients from rich volcanic ash.

Before the valley's fertile soil and climate were recognized in the 1950s, rail lines were built to transport the fruit and grains of the lower Yakima Valley. The North Coast Railroad was incorporated in 1906, and merged with the Oregon-Washington Railroad and Navigation Company, beginning operations in 1910. The Attalia to North Yakima line was then leased to Union Pacific on January 1, 1936. This line liberated the valley from the domination of The Northern Pacific Railroad and their line from Kiona to Yakima City.

Cleverly sculpted garbage cans in the shape of animals line the trail.

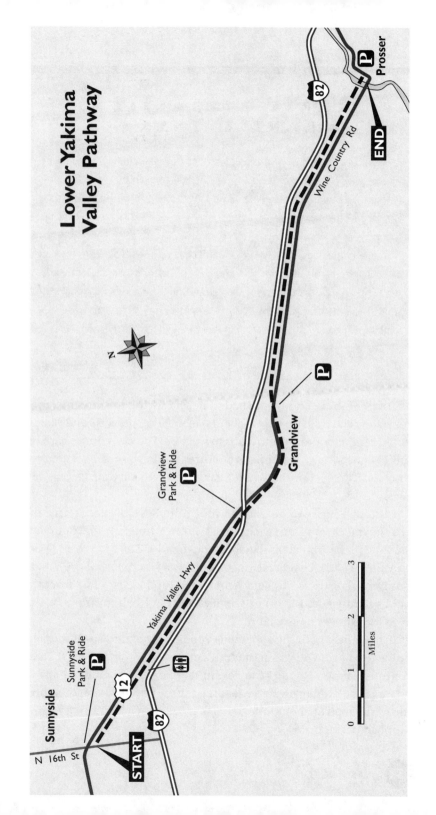

Lower Yakima
Valley Pathway

Prosser

82

Wine Country Rd

END

P

N

P

Grandview

Grandview
Park & Ride

P

Sunnyside
Park & Ride

P

Sunnyside

12

N 16th St

START

82

Yakima Valley Hwy

Miles

0   1   2   3

NEARBY ATTRACTIONS AND EVENTS

It's worth your while to visit the Lower Yakima Valley during a wine event. There's the Spring Barrel Tasting in April, Thanksgiving in the Wine Country (wines paired with appetizers), and Red Wine and Chocolate in February. Breweries offer tastings as well. Bring your bike booties or wool socks for fall and winter temperatures in the 30s.

Other amenities in the area include the golf course across from the trail at Sunnyside Park, the Yakima Electric Train Museum in the city of Yakima, the Columbia Gorge Discovery Center, and the Richland Educational Museum. The Lake Wallula Scenic River Hiking Trail (Trail 34) is across the Columbia in Oregon, about thirty minutes away. The Cowiche Canyon Trail (Trail 26) is near Yakima.

You'll be traveling in unshaded desert: Bring lots of sunscreen and water. The trail is narrow (about 8 feet wide)—cyclists and skaters should remember to be courteous to walkers. You can admire garbage cans disguised as cute animal sculptures while you relax on covered benches. The section between Grandview and Prosser has no services.

Although you can access the trail from several places, this description takes you from west to east. From Sunnyside to Grandview (6.5 miles), the trail is sandwiched between I–82 and Route 12 (Yakima Valley Road), beside fast-food spots, gas stations, and the town's commercial districts. Tuckers Winery and Produce is across from the trail in Sunnyside. For other winery locations, call the Yakima Valley Wine Growers Association.

A 1.5-mile gap in the trail takes you between the two Grandview trailheads. Once you reach the trail's end at Grandview Park & Ride, continue east on Route 12 to regain it. There's a shoulder most of the way. Look for an archway reading PALACIOS PARKWAY on the north side of the road at about mile 8. It's marked with a bench, water, and trailhead parking.

On your way through town, detour to the Dykstra House restaurant—a National Historic Site built in 1909—on Birch 1 block off the highway. Grandview is a farm workers' town, easygoing and friendly, and a good choice for real Mexican food.

The trail is newer and smoother much of the way from here to Prosser. Travel rural desert for almost 6 miles until Chukar Cherries appears. Do not pass go: Stop here for your gourmet sweet treat. Try wild Cascade blueberries coated with white chocolate, truffles, or Cabernet chocolate cherries. If you're lucky, you'll walk in on a tasting.

The trail has a touch of a grade here and there as you approach the desert mountains ahead. A new section of trail dips down from the right-of-way to navigate an active trestle crossing at mile 11.5. Cross the Yakima River 3 miles farther on. The trail merges with the sidewalk east of the river and ends here in downtown Prosser. The Benton County Museum is down the road. Check your winery map to attend a tasting.

Welcome to 37 miles of paved riverfront trail in a region that receives a meager 11 inches of rain per year. The sun shines on the Spokane River, rapids rush downriver, and bridges criss-cross the water. The Centennial Trail has three different personalities: the bustling and beautiful downtown Riverfront Park; the calm and gentle terrain to the east; and the hilly section high above the river, to the west. Both the eastern and western routes have sections on roadside shoulders. This is hot, desert country. Much of the trail is without services other than trail-head rest rooms, and water. Pack a snack and bring a water bottle to refill along the way. Benches and picnic tables offer rest stops beside the river.

Activities:

Location: Nine Mile Dam to the Idaho border, Spokane County

Length: 37 miles

Surface: Asphalt, with some sections on roadside shoulders. Though horses are allowed on the side of the trail its entire length, a soft trail parallels the trail from the state line to Barker Road.

Wheelchair access: Most of the trail is wheelchair accessible. The area west of downtown Spokane is quite hilly. Call the park for a list of accessible parking areas.

Difficulty: The trail ranges from easy to difficult; see the descriptions of each section.

Food: You'll find things to eat in downtown Spokane, at the Spokane Valley Mall, and at the Idaho border.

Rest rooms: There are many rest rooms along the trail. See map for approximate locations.

Seasons: The trail can be used year-round, although water is turned off and some rest rooms are closed from October through April.

Access and parking: You can access both the westbound and eastbound segments of the trail from Riverfront Park in downtown Spokane. Sontag Park on Charles Road and the Idaho border mark the western and eastern termini. Parking is available at most trailheads. For more information contact Riverside State Park (509) 456–2729.

Rentals: You can rent bicycles at Riverfront Park (800–336–PARK) and at bike shops on Division Street at the waterfront. Call the Spokane Visitor Center for more information.

Contact: Riverside State Park, (509) 456–8249, www.riversidestatepark.org; or Spokane Visitor Center, 888–SPOKANE, www.visitspokane.com

Bus routes: STA #20, 90, 82. For information, call (509) 328–RIDE or visit www.spokanetransit.com; also see the sidebar on page 159.

• •

W alla Walla was the state's largest city in 1800, but that reign was short-lived. By 1883, a nationwide rail connection was established in Spokane and the small town experienced a population explosion. In less than ten years, Spokane went from a city of 350 residents, to a population of 19,222, quadrupling the size of Walla Walla.

The legacy of the rails is evident throughout the Spokane Centennial Trail. Numerous railroads sketched a matrix of tracks in this area. The Inland Empire Railroad, owned by the local newspaper company, donated the trail from Argonne to the state line. Great Northern contributed the Don Kardong Bridge. Spokane's Great Northern Station sat on Havermade Island on the river.

Riverfront Park in downtown Spokane receives heavy use. This hundred-acre park blends a natural setting with a hearty history reflected in bridges, dams, and turn-of-the-twentieth-century buildings. Outdoor sculptures decorate the paths, from the amusement park and the Imax Theater to the century-old, hand-painted carousel. The rail-trail tours downtown hotels and runs just blocks from pubs, coffeehouses, restaurants, and shopping. The city turned the abandoned railroad tracks into this unique park and outdoor amusement center for the 1974 Expo.

You can use Riverfront Park to begin an exploration of the Centennial Trail that travels either west or east. The eastern trip is gentle and dry; to the west, look for hilly terrain. If you're new to this area, you'll learn about boulder fields and basalt cliffs, ice floods and aquifers. You'll also see exquisite homes and parks created by the

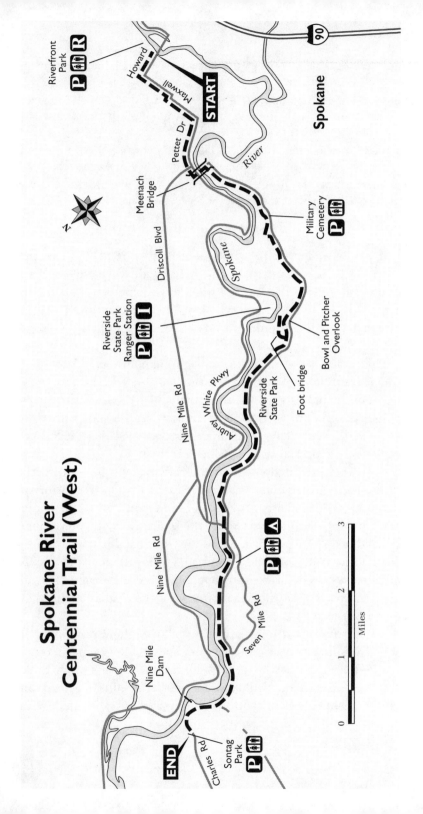

Spokane River
Centennial Trail (West)

Riverfront
Park

Howard

Maxwell

Pettet Dr

START

Spokane River

Spokane

Meenach
Bridge

Military
Cemetery

Driscoll Blvd

N

Spokane

Riverside State Park
Ranger Station

Nine Mile Rd

Aubrey White Pkwy

Bowl and Pitcher
Overlook

Riverside State Park

Foot bridge

Nine Mile Rd

Nine Mile
Dam

Seven Mile Rd

END

Charles Rd

Sontag Park

0   1   2   3
Miles

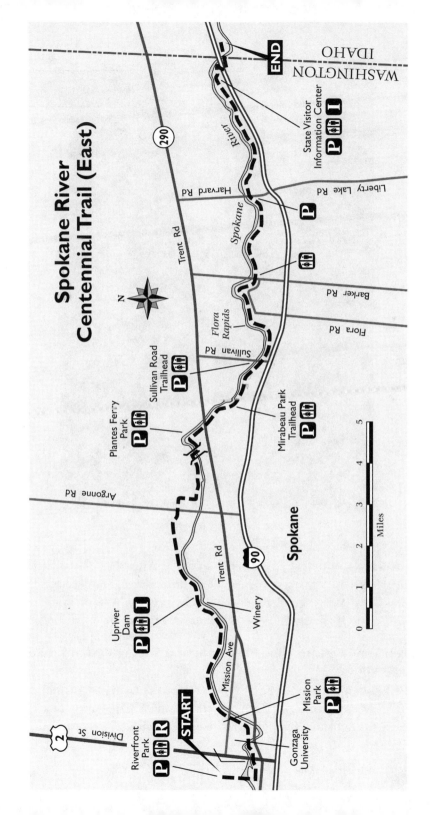

Spokane River Centennial Trail (East)

Upriver Dam

Riverfront Park

Division St

START

Mission Ave

Mission Park

Gonzaga University

Winery

Trent Rd

90

Spokane

Argonne Rd

Plantes Ferry Park

Sullivan Road Trailhead

Sullivan Rd

Flora Rapids

Mirabeau Park Trailhead

Trent Rd

290

N

Flora Rd

Barker Rd

Harvard Rd

Spokane River

Liberty Lake Rd

State Visitor Information Center

END

WASHINGTON
IDAHO

2

0 1 2 3 4 5

Miles

Trail view of Spokane and the suspension bridge in Riverside State Park.

prosperous mining of silver and gold and nurtured by the railroad. Check with the visitors bureau to locate homes, restaurants, bed-and-breakfasts, parks, and gardens reminiscent of the mining era. Stop at Patsy Clark's restaurant to enjoy wine and appetizers in the lounge.

Riverfront Park to Nine Mile Dam and Sontag Park, 14 miles westbound

The hilly route from the park west to Nine Mile Dam passes through ponderosa pines, horse pastures, and Riverside State Park lands, all beside the Spokane River. It's a rural area with no services. An eques-

TAKING THE BUS

A Spokane Transit Authority (STA) permit is required. You'll find the STA Plaza on Wall and Second Avenue. Watch a five-minute video on the second floor; no charge. Note that you can only do this 6:30 A.M. to 6:00 P.M. on weekdays, and limited hours on Saturday. Though permit systems are designed more for residents' needs than tourists', the bus drivers here are usually accommodating if it's your first time and you know how to load a bike. In exchange for their flexibility, they request that you be sure to warn them when you unload the bike. They don't want to run you over.

The #20 (Driscoll) bus from the STA Plaza takes you to Nine Mile Road, 5 miles from the western end of the trail. Leave the bus on Nine Mile Road at its last stop. Walk about 0.25 mile on the side of the road and turn left at the RIVERSIDE STATE PARK sign at Rifle Club Road. (Don't cross the street to ride the distance—no shoulders, fast traffic). Reach a T-intersection at Aubrey White Parkway. Turn left to reach the developed area of the park. From there, you can cross the footbridge and head up to the Centennial Trail on a dirt trail. Head straight from the steps on the south side of the river (don't take the first trail to the left).

Once you're in the woods, under the basalt cliffs, turn left on the short steep trail at the four-way intersection. You'll be on the main trail in about 0.5 mile from the bridge. For an alternate route, turn right onto Aubrey White Parkway. Enjoy a rolling ride on a small riverside road for about 2 miles to the dead end at the Seven Mile Road bridge crossing. Cross the bridge and pick up the trail at the signs on the south side of the bridge.

trian area lies adjacent. To reach the equestrian parking area at Trailpound Stables in Riverside State Park, take Seven Mile Road to Riverside Park Drive. Turn right and then turn again at the first right. The stable will be a 0.25 mile down the road. You can ride the road back to the Centennial Trail and use the paved trail or the soft shoulder.

To park at the military cemetery, cross the TJ Meenach Bridge from Pettit Road, which becomes Fort George Wright Road on the south side of the bridge. Turn right (west) at Government Way. After about 1 mile turn right on Houston Road to the lot. Horses can use the paved trail or the soft trail beside it.

There are also 10- and 25-mile loops for equestrians near the eastern terminus of the trail.

To ride the entire 14 miles, consider taking the bus from Spokane to Nine Mile Road, 5 miles from the western end of the trail, and riding back. The bus trip takes about thirty minutes and parallels some of the trail. For a short hike, start at the main entrance to Riverside State Park, cross the footbridge, and hike up to the trail.

To begin at Riverfront Park, exit the park on Howard Street near the Spokane Arena. You have about 2.5 miles of city-street travel ahead. Use caution: Drivers are not bicycle-savvy. Ride up Howard several blocks and turn left onto Maxwell. This turns into Pettét and heads down a steep hill. At Meenach Bridge, hop onto the sidewalk to curve up onto the bridge. It drops you onto the trail on the south side of the river. It's well signed. Watch for horse droppings through the equestrian area.

Wander through young pines and horse pasture, up and down hills. Pass a trailhead parking area at the military cemetery. Turn right onto Riverside State Park Road at the T-intersection at mile 29.5 (mile markers begin at the eastern terminus). The trail reaches a parking cul-de-sac and overlook above the Bowl and Pitcher rock formation and the suspension footbridge to Riverside State Park. The fun is yet to come. Head downhill 0.42 mile on the trail to a cairn on the right, across from the trail numbered 38. Take the trail to the right to reach the footbridge in 0.3 mile. Take the narrow, dirt trail to a four-way intersection. A right turn will take you to a bridge and a picnic shelter; a left will let you hang out on the rocks above the river or choose a rocky trail to the bridge. Hug the cliffs to pass between them on this route. Once you're on the bridge, the river rapids under your feet are a rush. This is your starting point if you parked at the main entrance to Riverside State Park on Aubrey White Parkway or took the #20 bus.

Once you're back on the main trail, pass through a burned area with a basalt ridge above and river rapids below. Several trails drop to the river along the way. Near mile 34, explore the history of Seven Mile Camp, a Civilian Conservation Corps operation of the 1930s.

The trail through Downtown Spokane.

The suspension footbridge is one of many accomplishments of this impressive group. Just beyond are the Wilbur Road Trailhead and a bit of trail on Aubrey White Parkway. Signs direct you to turn left onto Seven Mile Road, then make an immediate right onto Riverside State Park Drive. Enjoy the brief flat section before you cruise the hills to Nine Mile Dam.

You'll drop down to Deep Creek Bridge and a picnic area just past mile 36. There are plenty of benches and overlooks along the way. The best view is that of the gushing water released at Nine Mile Dam. From here, the trail crosses Charles Road to quickly end at Sontag Park. Unless you've planned a shuttle trip, turn around and return the way you came.

Riverfront Park to Idaho, 23 miles eastbound

The eastern half of the Centennial Trail is nothing like the west, except that it runs by the river. Once you leave downtown at Upriver Drive, a calm river follows close beside a gentle grade most of the way to Idaho. Pines decorate the desert landscape; the sun warms you.

Leave Riverfront Park on the south side of the river by the Trade Center and the Doubletree Hotel. Wind around a quiet residential area to the Don Kardong Bridge. The unmarked left turn across the bridge is just beyond milepost 22. This teal-colored trestle paints a pretty exit from the city. Cross up and over Hamilton Street on a pedestrian overpass or remain beside it on the trail. The handicapped-accessible trail turns left to cross the street at the light. Just beyond, cross Mission Avenue at Gonzaga University and follow signs to turn right onto the sidewalk and left onto the trail just before the river crossing. The trail has a bit of grade from here (noticeable for beginner skaters).

The city section gives way to the suburbs here. The trail lies on the roadside shoulder from mile 17.5 to mile 19.5 (Greene Street) and again from mile 13.5 to mile 16. The separated trail runs from mile 16 to mile 17 and again from the dead end of mile 13.5 (Maringo Drive) to Idaho. The dangerous roadside section is near Argonne Road (mile 14–16).

Pass the Arbor Crest Winery just past mile 18. The Upriver Dam is just ahead. A kiosk describes Spokane's search for clean water as the population grew in the early 1900s. The story of the aquifer that provides water to 300,000 residents is told here. Rock jocks and mountain bikers hang out at the Minnehaha Rocks at mile 17. This is one of the rock deposits dumped here from the collapse of the Purcell ice lobe, a 2,000-foot-high ice dam in Idaho. This glacial flood occurred at the tail end of the last ice age, 20,000 years ago.

At Boulder Beach, the trail continues on the road and up a hill 1.5 miles to Argonne Road. Continue straight through Argonne then turn right at the trail sign at Farr Road, a few blocks beyond. Turn left again onto Maringo. It ends quickly at a roadless, riverside trail. To avoid most of the road, start here. You can park at the Argonne Library at the corner of Argonne and Upriver. Check out the Rocket Bakery, also on Argonne.

Enjoy a wide, smoothly paved, scenic tour from Maringo to Mirabeau Park. Watch for deer, ospreys, and herons as you wander through the open pine forest. Cross the bridge at Plantes Ferry Park. Pause at the bench beside the secluded riverside. Skating is good from here all the way to Idaho. There are areas with some grade and one short narrow hill as you approach Mirabeau Park.

Pass under Trent Road or take the side trail up to Fitness Fanatics for a retail break at this skate shop.

Eastern section of the trail near Mirabeau Park.

Reach Sullivan Road past milepost 10 and wake up to the traffic of the Spokane Valley Mall. Here you can grab some food and a bus to downtown Spokane (I–90). This is the eastern terminus for weekend buses, in case you're looking for a ride back to town. A commuter bus reaches the Idaho border during the week. To find the Park & Ride, exit the trail at the Sullivan Road Trailhead and follow the sidewalk left across the river. The Park & Ride is several blocks down on the same side of the street. Fifty minutes will get you back to town.

From Sullivan Road, the trail returns to a rural riverside route with birds, boaters, and rapids. It opens up to a headwind 3 miles from the border. Cross under I–90 and over the river. You can continue into Idaho, 4.5 miles to Past Falls and beyond. The falls here are spectacular. The Idaho route to Coeur d'Alene switches from trail to roadside and has confusing spots. Contact Coeur d'Alene Parks at (208) 769–2252 for information.

MORE RAIL-TRAILS

A · Ben Burr Trail

The Ben Burr Trail is carved into a basalt rock outcropping above neighborhood homes. You'll find interesting geological formations here. The condominium building at Liberty Park is the old power-house for the electric railroad line.

Activities:

Location: City of Spokane, Spokane County

Length: 1.1 miles

Surface: Crushed stone, gravel, and dirt, rolled

Wheelchair access: The entire trail is wheelchair accessible.

Difficulty: Easy

Food: There are grocery stores several blocks from the trail.

Rest rooms: You'll find rest rooms and drinking water at both Liberty and Under Hill Parks.

Seasons: The trail can be used year-round.

Access and parking: To reach Liberty Park, take exit 283A (Altamount) off I-90 in Spokane. Turn right on Altamount and right on Fourth Street in 1 block. Turn left into Liberty Park; this lot is plowed when there's snow. You can also access the trail at Under Hill Park.

Rentals: You can rent bikes at Riverfront Park (800–336–PARK), skis and snowshoes at Mountain Gear, 2002 North Division Street in Spokane.

Contact: Spokane Parks and Recreation, (509) 625–6200; or Spokane Visitors Center, (888) SPOKANE.

Bus routes: None

B Colfax Trail

The remote and woodsy Colfax Trail follows the Palouse River for 3 miles. Cattle are pastured across the trail in a couple of areas; one bridge is unimproved and taken at the user's risk.

Activities:

Location: City of Colfax, Whitman County

Length: 3 miles

Surface: Dirt

Wheelchair access: This trail is not wheelchair accessible.

Difficulty: Easy

Food: No food is available along the Colfax Trail.

Rest rooms: There are no rest rooms along the trail.

Seasons: The trail can be used year-round.

Access and parking: From Colfax, take Highway 26 westbound for less than 1 mile, cross the bridge over the Palouse River, and take an immediate right onto Riverside Lane. Park just after the gravel pit on the right. The trail starts here, at the NO MOTORIZED VEHICLES sign. Please close all gates after passing through.

Rentals: No rentals are available near this trail.

Contact: Whitman County Parks, (509) 397–6238

Bus routes: None

C Dry Creek Trail

The Dry Creek Trail parallels Dry Creek and passes through pockets of old-growth timber. It starts out flat, then climbs; your total elevation gain is nearly 1,300 feet.

Activities:

Location: Gifford Pinchot National Forest in Skamania County, 15 miles north of the Columbia Gorge

Length: 4 miles

Surface: Dirt

Wheelchair access: The trail is not wheelchair accessible.

Difficulty: Moderate

Food: No food is available along the trail.

Rest rooms: There are rest rooms at the Trapper Creek Wilderness Trailhead.

Seasons: You can enjoy Dry Creek Trail from May through November.

Access and parking: Exit Route 14 at Wind River Highway in Carson. Drive 14 miles, past the Stabler Country Store. Turn right 1 mile after the Carson National Fish Hatchery, at a TRAPPER CREEK WILDERNESS sign. The road ends at the trailhead in approximately 1 mile.

Rentals: No rentals are available along this trail.

Contact: Wind River Information, (509) 427–3200, www.fs.fed.us/gpnf

Bus routes: None

Ⓓ Duwamish Bikeway

The north end of this trail sits at Alki Beach, the Venice (California) of Puget Sound, a beachfront with blades, bikes, and bronze volleyball bodies from here to there. Here, the trail is wide, flat, and smooth. It extends south to an industrial area along the Duwamish River. The link between these two sections, at Spokane Street, is incomplete and confusing and requires a brief trek on a busy road. The south end of the trail turns left at Michigan and forks at the First Avenue South Bridge. Turn south for 0.5 mile to the end of the trail at Holden Street. You can continue west onto the Alki Trail from 64th Avenue Southwest for about 2 miles. Kellogg Island is on West Marginal Way, south of Southwest Idaho Street. When the link between the Duwamish and Green River Trails is complete, you'll be able to travel from the Seattle waterfront to the Green River and connect to the King County Interurban Trail.

Activities:

Location: West Seattle to South Seattle, in King County

Length: 5 miles

Surface: Asphalt, with brief sections along the roadside.

Wheelchair access: The trail is wheelchair accessible.

Difficulty: Easy

Food: You'll find things to eat in the town of Alki.

Rest rooms: There are rest rooms at Alki Beach.

Seasons: The trail can be used year-round.

Access and parking: To reach the trail, take the West Seattle Bridge to the Harbor Avenue exit. Turn right. The sidewalk on your right is the trail. Drive as far north as you like and park on the street. You can also access the trail from Kellogg Island Park.

Rentals: See list of Puget Sound rentals.

Contact: City of Seattle Transportation Bicycle & Pedestrian Program, (206) 684–7583

Bus routes: For information on bus routes, call Metro Transit at (206) 553–3000 or visit transit.metrokc.gov.

Ⓔ Issaquah-Preston Trail

The scenic start on a wooden bridge over the East Fork of Issaquah Creek leads you down a wooded trail beside I–90. Eventually, when the new I–90 interchange is completed (three to four years from publication date), this trail will serve as a link between the Preston-Snoqualmie Trail, the Rainier Multiuse Trail, and the Sammamish Trail.

Activities:

Location: Issaquah and Preston, King County

Length: 2 miles

Surface: Ballast

Wheelchair access: The trail is not wheelchair accessible.

Difficulty: Easy

Food: No food is available near the trail.

Rest rooms: There are no rest rooms along the trail.

Seasons: The trail can be used year-round.

Access and parking: Take exit 20 (High Point Road) off I–90. Turn north and then left into the unmarked parking lot on the north edge of the I–90 on-ramp, westbound. This is the High Point Trailhead.

Rentals: See Puget Sound list of rentals.

Contact: King County Office of Open Space, (206) 296–7800

Bus routes: None

F John Wayne Pioneer Trail—Milwaukee Road Corridor

This segment of the John Wayne Pioneer Trail is an adventure. It passes through several geological zones, some with dramatic scenery and varied wildlife. The trail is undeveloped, has some difficult surfaces, and is sometimes confusing to navigate. A 40-mile gap from Royal Junction to Warden takes you on detours over county roads. A permit is required, and keys are loaned for access through gates. You may find snow for skiing and snowshoeing several weeks of the year—mostly from the Idaho border west about 20 miles. Fishing can be found on Department of Fish and Wildlife lands near the trail. Special permission is sometimes granted to cross the Columbia River on foot, on a bike, or on a horse at the Wanapum Dam or on the I–90 bridge.

Activities:

Location: Beverly to Tekoa, in Grant, Adams, and Whitman Counties

Length: 145 miles

Surface: Crushed stone, ballast, and dirt; the surface is deep and sandy for long sections of the trail.

Wheelchair access: The trail is not wheelchair accessible.

Difficulty: Easy to moderate. Though the trail is mostly flat, the surface can make for tough travel.

Food: You'll find food in the towns of Othello, Beverly, Lind, Rosalia, Warden, and Tekoa

Rest rooms: There are no rest rooms or drinking water along this trail.

Seasons: The trail can be used year-round.

Access and parking: To obtain information on the access points, present conditions, and permits, contact the DNR (see Contact). They will send a packet of information and maps.

Rentals: No rentals are available along this trail.

Contact: Washington Department of Natural Resources, Ellensburg, (509) 925–8510

Bus routes: None

G Middle Fork Trail

The Middle Fork Trail is a narrow pathway through a dense forest of western hemlock, around pockets of old growth, across bridges over wetlands and streams, and occasionally beside the Middle Fork of the Snoqualmie River. You'll travel beside the Alpine Lakes Wilderness and visit Goldmeyer Hot Springs for a soak. (Call first.) The terrain becomes more rugged in the upper reaches of the trail.

Activities:

Location: North Bend, King County

Length: 14.5 miles

Surface: Gravel, dirt, and clay

Wheelchair access: The trail is not wheelchair accessible.

Difficulty: Moderate; there are some narrow, steep sections.

Food: No food is available along the trail.

Rest rooms: You'll find rest rooms at the Middle Fork Trailhead.

Seasons: Although the trail can be used year-round, it's not maintained in winter.

Access and parking: Take exit 34 off I–90 (Edgewick Road). Turn north, drive 0.4 mile, then turn right onto Southeast Middle Fork Road (also called Southeast Lake Dorothy Road). The dirt Forest Service Road 5600 (not plowed in winter) takes you from mile 3 to the trailheads. You'll find the Middle Fork Trailhead 12.3 miles from I–90; Dingford Creek is 5.5 miles farther, and the unmarked Dutch Miller Gap access is located 1,200 feet before the end of the road. Cross the river on suspension bridges to the trail. Cross-country skiing is not recommended, but you can snowshoe from any point you can reach by car.

Rentals: No rentals are available along the trail.

Contact: U.S. Forest Service, North Bend, (425) 888–1431; or Goldmeyer Hot Springs, (206) 789–5631

Bus routes: None

Necklace Valley Trail

The Necklace Valley Trail is named for the loop of lakes it travels, which look like a jeweled necklace. It's a very steep trail; the railroad right-of-way portion of the trail extends for 1.5 miles. This portion was logged in the 1920s. Continue for 3.5 miles on a flat trail through old-growth forest, then climb steeply for the last 2.5 miles.

Activities:

Location: Mount Baker–Snoqualmie National Forest, King County

Length: 7.5 miles, 1.5 miles of which travel on the railroad right-of-way

Surface: Dirt

Wheelchair access: The trail is not wheelchair accessible.

Difficulty: Easy for 5 miles. Difficult for 2.5 miles

Food: No food is available along the trail.

Rest rooms: There are no rest rooms along the trail.

Seasons: The trail can be used year-round.

Access and parking: From Route 2, turn south on Foss River Road. Drive 4.1 miles to the Necklace Valley Trailhead on the left, signed TRAIL #1062. In winter the road is plowed up to the trestle, 1.5 miles from the highway.

Rentals: No rentals are available along the trail.

Contact: U.S. Forest Service, Skykomish Ranger Station, (360) 677–2414

Bus routes: None

Pacific Crest National Scenic Trail, Stevens Pass Right-of-Way Section

The Pacific Crest National Scenic Trail spans 2,000 miles. A 1.5-mile railroad right-of-way begins at Stevens Pass and follows the path of the upper switchback of the rail line. The trail then leaves the right of way and enters the Henry M. Jackson Wilderness Area.

Activities:

Location: Route 2, Stevens Pass, Chelan County

Length: 1.5 miles

Surface: Dirt

Wheelchair access: The trail is not wheelchair accessible.

Difficulty: Easy

Food: No food is available along the trail.

Rest rooms: There are no rest rooms along this trail.

Seasons: The trail can be used year-round.

Access and parking: The trail begins at Yodelin, the lot directly across from Stevens Pass Ski Area. It takes off from the east corner of the lot.

Rentals: No rentals are available along the trail.

Contact: U.S. Forest Service, Lake Wenatchee, (509) 763–3103

Bus routes: None

Ⓙ Rainier Multiuse Trail

The paved trail begins on Rainier Avenue Southeast at Gilman Boulevard, 1 block west of Front Street. It passes the community center, the historic railroad depot, the logging railroad display, the Skateboard Park, and the brewery and eateries of downtown Issaquah. After crossing Second Avenue, it becomes a narrow, undeveloped dirt-and-gravel trail that heads uphill behind the high school. At 1 mile, you'll reach a three-way intersection. The Rainier Trail drops down to the left onto Sunset Way. Eventually, the Rainier Multiuse Trail will cross I–90 to connect with the Issaquah-Preston Trail; look for this in several years, when the new interchange is completed.

Activities:

Location: Issaquah, King County

Length: 2.54 miles

Surface: 1.54 miles of the trail is paved; 1 mile is dirt and ballast

Wheelchair access: The paved portion of the trail is wheelchair accessible

Difficulty: Easy to difficult

Food: You'll find groceries and restaurants in the town of Issaquah.

Rest rooms: There are rest rooms at the Community Center.

Seasons: The trail can be used year-round.

Access and parking: Take exit 17 off I–90 and head south to Gilman Boulevard. Turn right on Gilman. Take the first left, onto Rainier Avenue Southeast, just past the chamber.

Rentals: See Puget Sound list of rentals

Contact: City of Issaquah, (425) 837–3322

Bus routes: None

This flat, paved trail lies in a peaceful park setting between the Fremont Bridge and Seattle Pacific University on the south side of the ship canal. The benches on the grassy waterfront, the shade of the willow trees, the boats slowly passing by, and the occasional rising of the bridge provide a relaxing stroll or skate. Cyclists use the trail as connection between city bike routes.

Activities:

Location: Seattle, King County

Length: 0.8 mile

Surface: Asphalt

Wheelchair access: The entire trail is wheelchair accessible.

Difficulty: Easy

Food: Try Ponti's Italian Seafood restaurant, or the Fremont eateries and breweries across the bridge.

Rest rooms: There are no rest rooms along this trail.

Seasons: The trail can be used year-round.

Access and parking: Park at Ewing Ming Park on Third Avenue West, 1 block north of West Nickerson Street, or on Nickerson. The trail runs from Sixth Avenue west to the Fremont Bridge.

Rentals: See Appendix A for a list of rentals in Puget Sound.

Contact: City of Seattle Transportation Bicycle and Pedestrian Program, (206) 684–7583

Bus routes: #17, #31. For more information, check out the Metro Transit Web site at transit.metrokc.gov, or call them at (206) 553–3000.

L Snoqualmie Centennial Trail

The Northwest Railroad Museum is the highlight of this trail. Pass old steam engines on the tracks, visit the museum, and take a train ride to the ledge above the famous Snoqualmie Falls in summer or during the Christmas holidays. Visit the elegant Salish Lodge just beyond the trail.

Activities:

Location: Snoqualmie, King County

Length: 0.6 mile

Surface: Asphalt

Wheelchair access: The entire trail is wheelchair accessible.

Difficulty: Easy

Food: You'll find restaurants in the town of Snoqualmie.

Rest rooms: There are rest rooms in town and at the museum.

Seasons: The trail can be used year-round.

Access and parking: Take I-90 to exit 31. Head north and follow Route 202 through North Bend and on to the town of Snoqualmie. You can park on the street near the Northwest Railroad Museum.

Rentals: See Appendix A for a list of rentals in Puget Sound.

Contact: City of Snoqualmie, (425) 831-5337

Bus routes: #209, #929. For more information, check out the Metro Transit Web site at transit.metrokc.gov, or call them at (206) 553-3000.

M West Tiger Railroad Grade

The West Tiger Railroad Grade lies deep within the boundaries of the Tiger Mountain Natural Resources Conservation Area. All trails in this half of Tiger Mountain are for hiking only. You can only reach this one after hiking other trails that begin from the street; the access trails are steeper than the West Tiger Railroad Grade itself. From the trailhead, take the main trail 0.25 mile to the first trail to the right (High School Trail). Then take the right fork to reach an old gate. Reach the Tradition Plateau in about 1 mile, fork right at the power-line corridor. Turn right again, to another trail intersection (signed) to the Poo Poo Point Trail; this intersects the West Tiger Railroad Grade in about 2 miles.

Activities:

Location: Tiger Mountain State Forest, Issaquah, King County

Length: 5.5 miles

Surface: Dirt and ballast

Wheelchair access: The trail is not wheelchair accessible.

Difficulty: Moderate, with one steep area

Food: No food is available along the trail.

Rest rooms: There are no rest rooms along the trail.

Seasons: The trail can be used year-round.

Access and parking: Take exit 17 (Front Street) off I–90 from either direction. Head south 0.7 mile to Sunset (light) and take a left. After 0.2 mile, turn right onto Second Avenue. Pull into the dirt lot on the left just beyond the high school in 0.8 mile.

Rentals: No local rentals are available.

Contact: Washington State Department of Natural Resources, (800) 527–3305

Bus routes: None

Rails-to-Trails

OREGON

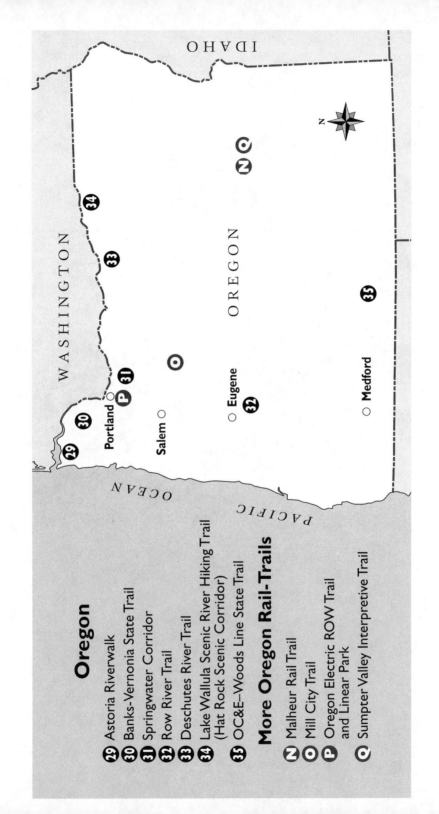

Oregon

29 Astoria Riverwalk
30 Banks–Vernonia State Trail
31 Springwater Corridor
32 Row River Trail
33 Deschutes River Trail
34 Lake Wallula Scenic River Hiking Trail
   (Hat Rock Scenic Corridor)
35 OC&E–Woods Line State Trail

More Oregon Rail-Trails

N Malheur Rail Trail
O Mill City Trail
P Oregon Electric ROW Trail
   and Linear Park
Q Sumpter Valley Interpretive Trail

INTRODUCTION

Though Oregon has only a few developed rail-trails, they run the gamut of terrain, scenery, and travel options. Some draw you to the state's most stunning sites; others combine with impressive light-rail and bus service to provide a commuter pathway. Tour forested foothills, riverside farmland, covered bridges, dams, and 100 miles of trail through mountains and river valleys. Pick a rural desert perch above the Columbia River, enjoy an oceanfront town, or follow the Deschutes River into a desert canyon. Travel beside towns buried underwater when dams were built.

Lewis and Clark reached Astoria in 1805, making this town the oldest settlement in the West. This beach resort town of the early 1900s sits on the northwestern tip of Oregon, where the Columbia River empties into the Pacific. The very civilized trail here entices you to stroll, ride, dine, and explore history. The Banks–Vernonia Trail, also west of Portland, is quite a contrast: It's a forested trek in the hills near tall trestles and railroad remnants between the tiny towns of Banks and Vernonia.

The Springwater Trail is part of a 40-mile loop around Portland and outlying areas. Combined with light-rail and bus service, this route provides a great leisure trip to Gresham and a commuter route with convenient, more passive options for the return trip. Botanical gardens and wildlife refuges near the trail replace the amusement parks that rallied railroad riders in the early 1900s.

The rich agriculture of the Willamette River Valley, from Portland south, drew the railroads up from California as early as 1870. The Row River Trail is the only rail-trail in this region. Enjoy the wildlife, wildflowers, and covered bridges as you travel alongside the river and the lake created by the dam.

The desert trails of eastern Oregon traverse above rivers and beside basalt rock walls. The trails in the Malheur National Forest hide you down in a draw and raise you to the highest point of the Sumpter Valley Railway. The rural Lake Wallula Trail sits high above the Columbia River, near the McNary Dam, and ends in riverfront parks. The Deschutes River Trail starts near the Columbia River Gorge and penetrates 18 miles into a desert canyon with ever-changing rock formations, high above the Deschutes River.

The OC&E–Woods Line State Trail, near the border of California, passes through small towns and climbs the old railroad switchbacks as it traverses 100 miles of diverse scenery and terrain.

Travel through history, natural beauty, and urban amenities on the rail-trails of Oregon. These trails are gifts that allow us to tour the state while we walk, skate, ski, or ride bikes and horses. Take advantage of them!

Oregon's

• • • • • • • • • • • • • • • • • •

TOP RAIL-TRAILS

29 Astoria Riverwalk

Portland's beach resort town of the early 1900s sits on the northwestern tip of Oregon, where the Columbia River empties into the Pacific Ocean. Lewis and Clark's 8,000-mile trek in search of the Northwest Passage brought them here in 1805, making this town the West's oldest American settlement and a National Historic District. Later, the Spokane, Portland & Seattle Railway brought cityfolk to the beach on Friday night for a weekend on the coast. Today bridges and boardwalks, canneries and cafes, docks and decks, galleries and espresso stops decorate the riverfront with history, views, and yuppie delights.

Activities: 🚶 🚲 🎣 🚴 🛼 🐦 🦌 🏃

Location: Smith Point to Tongue Point, Astoria, in Clatsop County

Length: 5.1 miles, 3 of which are fully developed (from 6th to 41st Street)

Surface: The developed portion is paved or planked trestles. The trestles are filled with ballast east of 41st; west of 6th Street, they're open.

Wheelchair access: The developed section of the trail is wheelchair accessible.

Difficulty: Easy; west of 6th Street, however, the open trestles are hazardous.

Food: You'll find things to eat in downtown Astoria.

Rest rooms: You'll find facilities at the foot of 39th Street, the Dough Boy Monument, and city public buildings.

Seasons: The trail can be used year-round.

Access and parking: To reach the trail, drive Route 101 to Astoria. From I–5 in Washington, exit at Longview, cross the Columbia River, and head west on Route 30. From Portland take Route 30 west. From the south, take Route 101 north. The trail is easily accessed anywhere along its length: Any numbered street from 6th to 41st ends at the river's edge and the trail. Park on the street.

Rentals: To rent bicycles, check out Hauer's Cyclery Shop at the foot of 16th Street (1606 Marine Drive in Astoria), or Bikes and Beyond at 11th Street and Marine Drive.

Contacts: City of Astoria, (503) 325–5821; Chamber of Commerce, (503) 325–6311

Bus routes: A restored city trolley runs from the western trail terminus at Smith Point to 39th Street daily in summer, and on weekends in winter. You can flag it down at any point.

• •

The Astoria Riverwalk Trail invites you to savor the sights, sounds, and tastes of a fun town while the historic buildings, fort, and monuments paint a picture of the earliest days of pioneering on the West Coast. Route 101, the coastal highway, is a busy street loaded with commercial activity. The Riverwalk lets you avoid this main drag and explore on foot, on a bike, or quite easily in a wheelchair. You can access this trail from almost anywhere and design a tour of your own.

The downtown section from 6th Street to 17th Street is more formal, with benches, lighting, and interpretive kiosks. It meanders

A restored trolley runs along the trail from the western trail terminus to 39th Street.

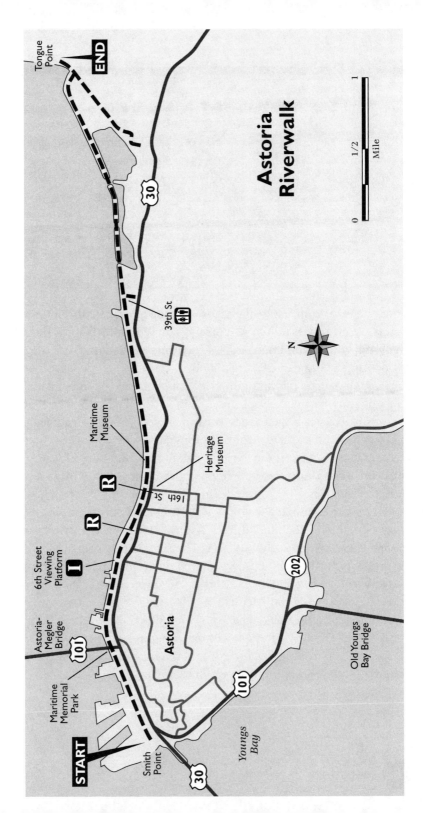

Tongue Point

END

30

Astoria Riverwalk

0   1/2   1
     Mile

39th St

N

Maritime Museum

Heritage Museum

16th St

R

R

6th Street Viewing Platform

I

Astoria-Megler Bridge

101

Maritime Memorial Park

START

Smith Point

Astoria

202

101

30

Youngs Bay

Old Youngs Bay Bridge

NEARBY ATTRACTIONS

Climb the 164 steps to the observation deck of the Astoria Column for a panoramic view of the region. The neighboring town of Warrenton has a waterfront trail and an eagle sanctuary. Nearby scenic locations include Long Beach Peninsula (famous for cranberries), and Seaside on the Oregon coast. Nearby rail-trails include the Raymond to South Bend Riverfront Trail to the north (Trail 23) and the Banks-Vernonia Trail toward Portland (Trail 30). Call the chamber (see "Contact") for its guide to the city and events.

along the riverfront with easy access to shops, restaurants, and museums. From 17th Street to 41st Street, you'll find a 10-foot-wide asphalt trail with fewer amenities. Use extreme caution on the trestles; the open ties here can capture a foot.

Though Astoria has an impressive list of claims to fame, its most amazing may be the sight of the Columbia River disappearing into the ocean. The 4.1-mile drive to Washington over the Astoria-Megler Bridge offers great views from the longest continuous three-span through-truss bridge in the world. The shore is one of ten locations between Alaska and Mexico where more than 100,000 birds may gather at one time. Try a visit during fall migration.

For a unique tourist attraction, watch a "bar pilot" leap from a tug onto a freighter to be guided in to Astoria. This is the only city on the West Coast where you'll see this. The river bar that separates the Columbia from the Pacific is considered one of the most dangerous in the world. It is said to have claimed 233 shipwrecks at the bottom of the "Graveyard of the Pacific."

If you hear a chorus of sea lions, look down to see them below the trestles. The city offers kayaking, canoeing, surfing, waterskiing, fishing, clamming, boat tours, and rail-bike tours. When you're done recreating, stop at the state's first brewery.

The Banks-Vernonia Trail stretches through the hills east of the Coast Mountains. It's 35 miles west of Portland, and 52 miles east of the coastal town of Seaside. Both trail endpoints—at Banks and at Vernonia—are paved for several miles, mostly along the highway. As you approach the middle third of the trail, it leaves the road and climbs into the forested hills on a gravel-and-ballast surface. Here you enter a different world. Miles of side trails create an outdoor museum of railroad relics, including an old section cabin. Look up at two 90-foot-high, 680-foot-long trestles. Enjoy views of the Coastal Range. Listen for an owl. You might see a fox, an elk, a deer, or a great blue heron.

Activities:

Location: The towns of Banks and Vernonia, in Columbia and Washington Counties

Length: 21 miles

Surface: 12 miles of the trail is asphalt, 9 miles gravel.

Wheelchair access: Wheelchair access is available on the trail's paved portions and at parks.

Difficulty: Easy to moderate, with difficult sections. The steep, potentially muddy descent to the highway at the Tophill Trailhead can be tough, and some areas have heavy gravel that's challenging even on a mountain bike. The trail has a 2 to 5 percent grade.

Food: The small town of Vernonia has a pub. The area just west of the junction of Routes 26 and 47 has a market, a restaurant, and gas station mini marts.

Rest rooms: There are vault and chemical toilets at all the trailheads except Manning.

Seasons: The trail can be used year-round.

Access and parking: To start in Vernonia, take Route 26 from Seaside or Portland to Route 47. If you're coming from Portland, head north 15 miles on Route 47; from Seaside, drive 11 miles north on a small unmarked road west of Route 47 signed TO VERNONIA. Stop at City Hall for a map. Turn south at the railroad engine on Adams Street in town. Park in Anderson Park; there's an interpretive kiosk here, as well as hitching posts.

The Beaver Creek Trailhead is found on Route 47 just over 4 miles south of Anderson Park; the Tophill Trailhead (with hitching posts), also on Route 47, is about 8 miles south. You'll have to make a steep uphill climb whether you start here or just pass through this part of the trail. The park manager's office and an interpretive trail are located at the Buxton Trailhead. To reach this trailhead, turn north on Fisher Road from Route 26, 0.5 mile east of the intersection with Route 47. Follow signs to the park. The Manning Trailhead is also on Route 26, 1 mile east of Route 47. This is the southernmost trailhead, 3.3 miles from the trail's end.

Rentals: None closer than Portland (See information for Springwater Corridor on page 189).

Contacts: Buxton Park Ranger, (503) 324–0606. For information on fishing and camping along the trail, call Lee's YouCatch, (503) 429–2450.

Bus routes: None

• • • • • • • • • • • • • • • • • • • •

The Spokane, Portland & Seattle Railway built the Gales Creek & Wilson River line in 1922. Other railroads refused to build a line expressly for hauling lumber, so this one was created to move timber products from northwestern Oregon, and in particular from the Oregon-American lumber mill in Vernonia. The trains also carried freight and passengers from Keasey to Portland. The line ceased to operate when the mill closed in 1957. The Vernonia South Park & Sunset Railroad leased the line and operated a steam sight-seeing train from 1960 to 1965. Abandoned in 1973, the rails were salvaged and the right-of-way sold to the state highway department. In 1990 it became the first linear state park in Oregon.

Five trailheads allow for easy access and trips of various lengths on paved or gravel surfaces. When you choose your starting point, keep in mind that the trail runs downhill from Vernonia on a 2 to 5 percent grade. Cyclists are asked to ride on one side, equestrians on the other. The grade may tempt you to cruise downhill on a bike; if so, pay attention to avoid collisions. Cyclists must yield to all users, and hikers must yield to horses. The paved areas of the trail are not ideal for skating; on the unpaved portions, a mountain bike works best.

This description takes you from Anderson Park in Vernonia southward. In Vernonia, the Banks-Vernonia Trail will eventually connect to the paved loop around Lake Vernonia, creating a lakeside trail-

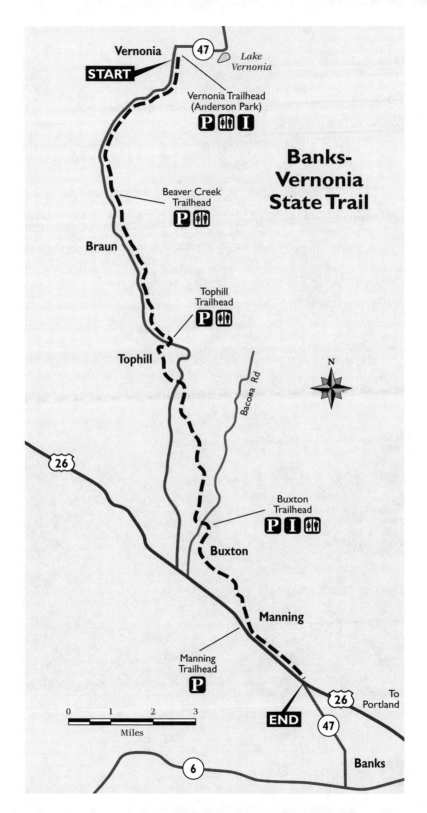

Vernonia

47

Lake Vernonia

START

Vernonia Trailhead
(Anderson Park)
P 🚻 I

Beaver Creek
Trailhead
P 🚻

**Banks-
Vernonia
State Trail**

Braun

Tophill
Trailhead
P 🚻

Tophill

Bacona Rd

N

26

Buxton
Trailhead
P I 🚻

Buxton

Manning

Manning
Trailhead
P

0   1   2   3
Miles

END

47

26

To
Portland

6

Banks

head. After you leave the park, the trail is paved for 7 miles, with a gravel path for horses. It parallels Route 47 and Beaver Creek until the shrubs and fir separate you from the highway. Good access to the Newhalem River for fishing can be found about 1 mile south of Vernonia and at Lee's YouCatch.

The trail leaves open areas lined with blackberry bushes and deciduous trees at mile 7, becomes dirt and gravel, and climbs into a forest of Douglas fir. A fossil bed located between miles 7 and 8 provides education for schoolchildren. As you approach the Tophill Trailhead, prepare for a steep descent to Route 47, where the burned Horseshoe Trestle forces trail users to cross the highway. Use caution.

A short climb returns you to the original grade. Detour left where the trail levels out to stand at the edge the 90-foot-high Horseshoe Trestle. It was 680 feet long before the other end fell victim to a fire. Indeed, fires plagued the construction of this portion of railway from the very start.

Turn right to follow the trail into deep forest. Cross the highway at milepost 10 and prepare for a group of historic side trips. Take the first fork to the left for 0.6 mile to see ruins of the longest trestle,

The Banks-Vernonia passes through the forested hills east of the Coast Mountains.

Take a side trip to see this burned-out trestle.

reported to be 1,000 feet long, and telegraph poles from the 1920s, still standing.

At milepost 12, hitch your horse or park your bike and walk to the old section cabin. Picture the railroad crew cooking on the wood-stove inside. At milepost 12.5, find another side trail, which crosses the main trail after 0.5 mile and crosses it again to become a short, fun single-track. These short, historic side trails built by the ranger and his volunteers total 10 additional miles.

Just past mile 13, you'll find an open area with picnic tables and hitching posts, built by the Oregon Youth Conservation Corps. Arrive at Buxton State Park to enjoy the grassy area and the pond stocked with newts, turtles, and frogs. Here 5,000 children learn about the ecosystem each year.

At milepost 15, Pongratz Road, detour onto 1.5 miles of dirt county road. At the T-intersection with Phil Road, a right turn takes you to the Manning Trailhead. Heading east, the trail dead-ends in the brush 0.25 mile from Banks.

If you ask nicely, the folks at the gas station at the intersection of Routes 26 and 47 may let you have my special "Wake-Up-and-Fill-Up Postride Mix": hot chocolate, French vanilla, and espresso.

When you've explored the trail to your heart's content, turn around and return the way you came. If your trip home takes you westward, visit the largest sitka spruce in the United States, on display on Route 26. If you're returning to Portland, check out the Northwest 23rd district off Burnside and Northwest 23rd Street for funky cafes and trendy shops. If you're on a rail-trail roll, check out the Astoria Riverwalk (Trail 29) or Portland's Springwater Corridor (Trail 31).

31 Springwater Corridor

The Springwater Corridor is the major southeast section of a system of nature trails encircling Portland. Ride, walk, or skate the trail to enjoy parks, botanical gardens, and wetlands—not to mention herons, coyotes, and deer—as you travel through industrial, suburban, and rural areas. August is blackberry month; don't hesitate to savor your way down the trail.

Activities:

Location: Portland to Boring, in Multnomah and Clackamas Counties

Length: 16.5 miles

Surface: Mostly asphalt, although 3 miles from Gresham to Boring are dirt.

Wheelchair access: The paved portion of the trail is wheelchair accessible.

Difficulty: Easy

Food: You'll find things to eat at several spots along the trail and in downtown Gresham

Rest rooms: There are rest rooms at Gresham Main City Park, at Tideman Johnson Park, and along the trail east of milepost 13.

Seasons: The trail can be used year-round.

Access and parking: To start at the west end, head to Tideman Johnson Park; park at Southeast Johnson Creek Boulevard and Southeast 45th. Three miles from the trail's eastern terminus, you can leave your car near Gresham Main City Park on Route 26 and South Main Avenue, or at the trailhead at Hogan Avenue, south of 19th Street, in Gresham.

Note that mileage markers reflect a trail start at a future trailhead at the west end. The Tideman Johnson Trailhead is at milepost 5. You can backtrack a couple of miles to enjoy this six-acre wilderness park.

Rentals: You can rent bikes from Fat Tire Farm at 2714 Northwest Thurman in Portland (503–222–3276)

Contact:
- Portland Parks and Recreation, (503) 823–PLAY, www.parks.ci.portland.or.us/Trails/SpringwaterCorridor/Swaterwelcome.htm
- Portland Visitor Center, (877) 678–5263, www.pova.com
- Gresham Visitor Center, (503) 665–1131

Bus routes: #9, #4, #84, or MAX (see the sidebar on page 192 for information on this light rail system)

• •

The Springwater Corridor consists of 16.5 miles of the 40-mile loop around the greater Portland area, a path first conceived of in 1903 to serve as a nature trail encircling the city. Though our forefathers lived in a city of woodlands and meadows, they had the foresight to plan this park and trail system, now slated to ultimately extend for 140 miles. This trail loop will connect three rivers and thirty parks, including 5 miles of the Columbia Slough suitable for canoeing, and an equestrian loop. A 10.8-mile section from south of Boring to Estacada may link the trail to the Pacific Crest Trail (a route from Mexico to Canada).

The Springwater Division Line of 1903 reached peak usage in 1906. Portland General Electric and the Portland Railway Light & Power Companies had six electric plants and 161 miles of rail, carrying 16,000 passengers each year and hauling farm produce to Portland markets. Towns popped up along the line; the railroad rallied ridership further by building amusement parks. Thousands of weekend passengers rode the rail to destinations such as the Oaks Amuse-

Tideman Johnson Park provides a lovely backdrop for a leisurely ride on the Springwater Corridor. (Courtesy Portland Parks and Recreation)

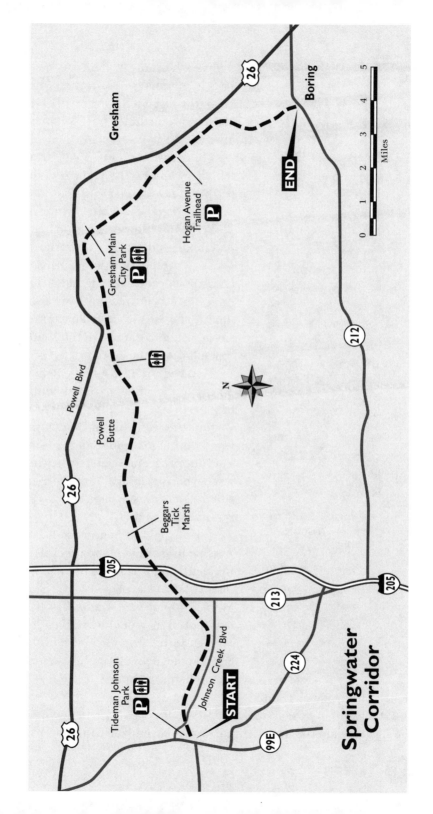

Springwater Corridor

Another result of Portland's prowess for planning is the city's light rail system, the MAX. This system allows you to bike, roll, or stroll the Springwater Corridor as far east as Gresham and Boring, then return easily via bus or rail. You must buy a Tri-Met pass to board your bike on MAX or a bus. It costs $5.00 and requires watching a fifteen-minute video at a bike shop or the Tri-Met office. This makes it tough for tourists, and drivers will not let you board without it. Plan ahead. The video advises of travel restrictions. (Please give the city feedback on how the system might be improved for you as a tourist.)

For more information on the light rail system, visit www.tri-met.org or call (503) 238–RIDE. For bike/bus info, call (503) 239–3044.

ment Park on the Willamette River. Passenger service continued until 1958; the city took over in 1990. In 1996 the Portland trail segment opened.

There are several spots from which to access the trail; this description takes you from Tideman Johnson Park eastward. From the park, the trail runs east beside roads in a mildly industrial neighborhood. Cross to the north side of Johnson Creek Boulevard at Southeast Bell Avenue for a brief respite from road noise. The Springwater Restaurant sits adjacent to the trail at the Southeast 82nd Avenue crossing.

Find Beggars Tick Wildlife Refuge on the left at milepost 11, at Southeast 111th Avenue. Take a break to wander the wetlands and watch the wood ducks, teals, and mergansers. Find one of several sheltered benches just beyond the refuge. These shelters suit the Northwest, where drizzle can set in at any time.

Take a right at Southeast 122nd Avenue for several blocks to explore five acres and 1,500 species of native plants at the Leach Botanical Garden. Mile 12.5 places you adjacent to a 630-foot-high volcanic rise called Powell Butte. Stop for views of the city and the mountains; a hike among the orchards, meadows, and forest; a picnic; or horseback riding.

Hills begin to appear and civilization disappears (for a while) as you head toward the mountains. Cross a peaceful creek at mile 13.5

and find those great covered benches just beyond. If you've been waiting for a rest room, here's your chance. If you're tired, consider this: The former Linneman Rail Station was named for a pioneer couple who navigated the Oregon Trail by ox cart in 1852. Bikes, walking shoes, and pavement seem quite the luxury compared to dirt, rocks, and oxen.

Pass beside Powell and under Southwest Eastman Parkway on your way to Main City Park in Gresham. Exit at the park to explore the eateries of Gresham on a pedestrian walkway and catch the bus or MAX back to Portland. It's fun to arrive for an evening out. Exit the trail through the park to Main Avenue. Cross Route 26/Powell Boulevard and continue on Main to 10th. Cross the tracks to the transit center. Check out the restaurants on Main Avenue. Then relax on your bus ride home.

To complete the trail, continue for another 2 miles on pavement, then 3 miles on dirt, to reach Boring. Boring Junction is the last remaining ticketing station of the Springwater Corridor. From Boring, take the #84 bus back to Gresham.

Portland is a great city blessed with amenities such as a rose garden, a paved waterfront trail, and great food. Explore.

> *"Parks should be connected and approached by boulevards and parkways....The system of scenic reservations, parks and parkways and connecting boulevards would ... form an admirable park system for such an important city as Portland is bound to become."*
>
> —The Olmstead brothers, landscape architects, 1904 (the same family designed Spokane's original parks)

32 Row River Trail

This abandoned railroad line left us five Howe truss bridges and twenty-three pile trestles to cross. Ospreys and eagles, a small town, covered bridges, and prairie wildflowers will delight you as you tour the scenic right-of-way. With more than twenty covered bridges, Lane County has more of these scenic spans than any other county west of the Appalachians.

Activities:

Location: Cottage Grove, 25 miles south of Eugene, in Lane County

Length: 15.6 miles

Surface: 12.6 miles is asphalt and quarter-inch gravel for horses. The remaining, undeveloped 3 miles is large ballast.

Wheelchair access: This trail is not wheelchair accessible.

Difficulty: Easy, although there's 1 mile of hills that may be tough for beginner skaters.

Food: You'll find things to eat in the town of Dorena.

Rest rooms: There are toilets at the Mosby Creek Trailhead and at Dorena Dam, Harms Park, Bake Stewart Park, and Dorena. Mosby Creek has drinking water.

Seasons: The trail can be used year-round.

Access and parking: To reach the western trailhead, Mosby Creek, take exit 174 off I–5 at Row River Road in Cottage Grove. Drive 2.5 miles southeast to Layng Road and the Currin Covered Bridge. Turn right, crossing Mosby Creek. Turn into the trailhead at 200 yards. The Mosby Creek Covered Bridge, built in 1920, is the oldest remaining covered bridge in Lane County.

Other trailheads are all found on Row River Road. These include Dorena Dam, Harms Park, Bake Stewart Park, and Dorena.

Rentals: No local rentals are available. Eugene and Springfield, 25 miles away, have bike shops.

Contact: Bureau of Land Management, Eugene, (541) 683–6600, www.edo. or.blm.gov/rec/row_trail

Bus routes: None

- -

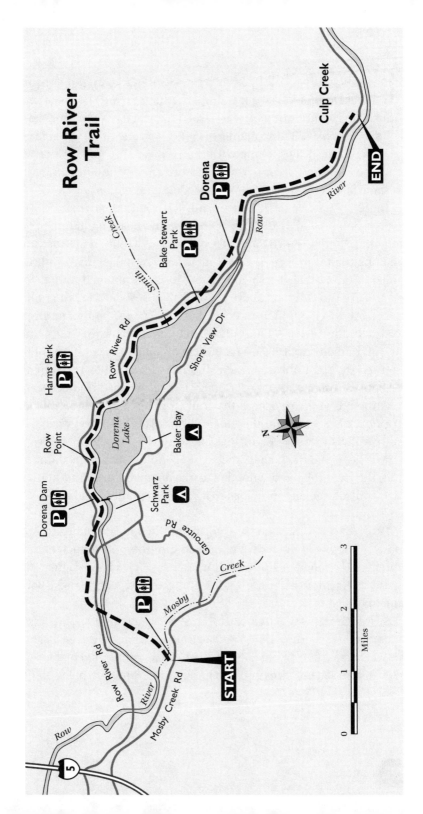

The Row River Trail passes by the Dorena Dam and runs beside Dorena Lake as it follows the Row River. The river (pronounced to rhyme with *cow*) was named for a fatal brawl over grazing rights in the 1850s. The Willamette Valley was one of the great farming areas in the 1880s, along with the Palouse and Walla Walla Valleys. These eastern areas of the state were already building railroads for their farm products. The West needed to move its goods.

In 1883 the Oregon & California Railroad constructed a line through Salem, and in 1902 the "Old Slow and Easy" main line of the Oregon & South Eastern Railroad Company was built. It ran ore from the Bohemia mining district as well as logs, supplies, mail, and passengers from Cottage Grove to Disston, in the Umpqua National Forest. In 1914 the Oregon Pacific & Eastern took over. Though regular passenger service ended in July 1930, the *Goose* hauled summer tourists in the 1970s. A handful of runs served the Culp Creek lumber mill into the late 1980s. The Bureau of Land Management (BLM) acquired the right-of-way in 1993 and paved it in 1996. The remaining 3 miles, through the city of Cottage Grove, will be developed soon.

Although you can access the trail from several points, this description takes you from the Mosby Creek Trailhead eastward. The trail parallels the Row River Road most of the way. You'll arrive at Dorena Dam and the lake it created at 3.5 miles. Before the dam was built, the river repeatedly flooded towns downstream. In addition to flood control, the dam provides irrigation, recreation, and improved navigation.

Look for a spring shout of color from the delicate plants at Row Point, remnants of the native prairie community. Please leave them protected so they can survive. At mile 5.3, see if you recognize the trestle at Harms Park, immortalized in the movies of Ernest Borgnine and Buster Keaton.

Smith Creek is an area of streams, marshes, and canary grass fields. Ospreys, herons, ducks, and geese are commonly seen. A keen eye may also catch a bald eagle, a deer, or the occasional black bear. You can also see the remains of an early settler's orchard below Smith Creek Bridge.

The trail runs beside the Dorena Reservoir. (Courtesy Bureau of Land Management (BLM) Eugene, Oregon)

Bake Stewart Park is named for two lilies; a poisonous one and an edible one. The bulb of the blue flowering lily was once dug up in early spring and baked in earth ovens for winter storage, while the white or "death" camas lilies were carefully avoided.

Arrive at the postdam town of Dorena at mile 12.5. Established in 1899, the original townsite included a church, dance hall, post office, store, blacksmith shop, and grocery, all located near the center of the present reservoir. To prepare for the dam, a portion of the railway and some buildings were moved. Others were burned prior to the filling of the reservoir in the 1940s. The old railroad route can be seen along the lake bottom during winter drawdown.

The eastern terminus of the trail, Culp Creek, was one of twenty mill towns along the railway. Before the railroad, logs went to mill via "river rats." These fellows made quite a wage riding the logs downriver to the mills. The railroad put an end to these wild and risky rides. The last mill disappeared a decade ago.

Whenever you're ready, turn around and return the way you came.

33 Deschutes River Trail

Take a scenic desert tour in a canyon above the Deschutes River. Visit the Columbia Gorge, Hood River, Goldendale, and the Dalles, and you've got an aesthetic, tasty, and interesting weekend. The canyon is hot, somewhat rocky, and occasionally sandy. It's a pretty flat trail that offers a slight downhill grade on the return. There are some nifty features along the way, including a constant view of the river.

Activities: 🚶 🏇 🚲 🦃 🐟 ⛺ 🦌 🎒

Location: Deschutes State Park at the Columbia River, Wasco, in Sherman County

Length: 18 miles

Surface: Dirt and gravel

Wheelchair access: The trail is not wheelchair accessible.

Difficulty: Easy, although in several spots the gravel may be difficult to ride on a bike.

Food: There are vending machines in the park.

Rest rooms: Public rest rooms and drinking water are available at the park.

Seasons: The trail is open year-round for hikers and bikers; it's open from March 1 through June 30 for equestrians.

Access and parking: Take exit 104 off I–84. Park signs point you south of the highway. Turn right (west) at the stop sign at the frontage road in the corner town of Biggs. Turn left into Deschutes State Park at just under 5 miles. You can park here at the park entrance and head through the gate from the parking area. Or drive to the end of the park road and travel across the grassy area that extends from the parking strip. Follow the sign up a steep narrow trail to the upper trail. This is the main trail.

Rentals: There are no rentals available near the trail.

Contact: Deschutes State Park, (541) 739–2322; or Oregon State Parks, (800) 551–6949, www.prd.state.or.us

Bus routes: None

• •

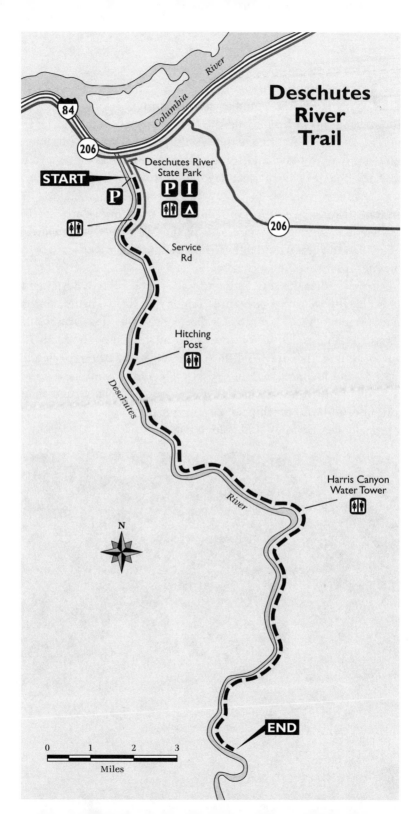

On the Deschutes River Trail, you're in the desert. You'll have hot, dry weather and little shade most of the year. There are no roads and no water beyond the park (except, of course, the river). The Department of Fish and Wildlife provides a few outhouses and two horse troughs, and some old boxcars have been renovated for shade. Still, to have a great day here, bring a hefty supply of water in insulated containers, heavy-duty sunscreen, and snacks. Try the trail in spring when lupine and other wildflowers are out, the weather is moderate, the pale hair of the big-horned sheep stands out against the green, and folks from west of the Cascades are ready for relief from the winter soak.

Also note that the trail is dotted with special plants designed to flatten bike tires, called puncture vine or goat heads. Bring an extra tube and a patch kit. If you get a flat, check your tire carefully for other three-thorned vines waiting to flatten you down the road. The Department of Fish and Wildlife sprays the area and removes huge bags of them for the safety of cyclists. The department also does a great job of providing habitat for birds, deer, and big-horned sheep along the trail and on the ridgetops. You may see western meadowlarks, doves, ospreys, and golden eagles.

The desert canyon walls of the Deschutes River Trail.

In addition to the main, upper trail that you'll be on, two lower walking trails run closer to the river for 2 miles. Anglers bike out or walk the lower trail to fish for steelhead from the banks of the Deschutes. Several paths along the main trail lead down to the river. The first 3 miles are in the state park; the next 15 are in Fish and Wildlife lands. The trail ends at a washout, which marks the start of Bureau of Land Management land.

From your perch on the trail, the canyon displays changing rock formations and views of the river. Magpies fly by, showing their striking black on white. Small birds and butterflies disperse as you disrupt the occasional drinking puddle.

You may see a train heading for Bend on the active line across the river. This western line, and the right-of-way you'll travel, were built by fierce competition. After receiving approval in 1906, two railroad companies—Hill's Oregon Trunk (OT) and Harriman's Des Chutes Railroad Company—went head to head in 1908 in a violent and political battle. The Oregon Trunk was a subsidiary of the Seattle, Portland & Spokane Railway, which was itself a subsidiary of the Northern Pacific and the Great Northern. Harriman's project was a subsidiary of the Oregon-Washington Railroad & Navigation Company, a Union Pacific company. The battle ended October 5, 1911, in Bend when seventy-three-year-old James Hill drove home the golden spike in two blows. The Des Chutes Railway, where the trail runs, built 95 miles of track, into Metolius. It used the Oregon Trunk trackage for routes from Metolius to Bend. The 156 miles of OT track is still used.

Trail mileage is well marked. The terrain drops into the river from the trail, presenting a dramatic view. At 3.5 miles, a dirt road provides access to the river, a picnic table, and an outhouse. Uphill from the trail, natural springs irrigate a cluster of shade trees. Cross a bridge built over a washout and find a horse trough at mile 4.5. Though a trail meanders downhill, it does not reach the riverside outhouse for boaters and anglers. Wait until mile 5.5, where a hitching post marks a trail to another outhouse. A renovated boxcar just beyond provides shade, a bit of history, or even a campsite. A small old wooden trestle and a rock wall built by Chinese railroad workers appear at mile 6. At mile 8 drop to the river for a swim, some shade, or a trip to the outhouse. Check out the boxcar. Climb the steps to cross the fence.

From here, the canyon widens and flattens. You might see a lonely cow grazing across the river. At 10 miles the trail approaches the Deschutes at a spot where towering rock formations jut out across the water. At mile 11, out of the barren hills emerge golden wheat and barley fields, followed by the old Harris homestead and a wooden water tower. The Department of Fish and Wildlife plants grains here to provide upland bird habitat (pheasant, quail, chukar) and deer and elk foraging. It also plants cottonwood trees for shade and for the birds—but no sooner are they planted than the beavers arrive in herds of twenty or more to chow down. Beware: The grasses hide rattlers, bull snakes, and nestling fawns.

Find some shade and rest on couches placed on the deck of an old building, and a trough for horses. At the water tower, find a trail to Harris Canyon that merges with other trails. Search for the hieroglyphics of Native Americans on rock walls in Harris Canyon.

Most travelers turn around at the Harris Ranch, because the trail beyond it is more remote. Washouts from the floods of 1995 and 1996 have recently been repaired with bridges covered by heavy gravel. Most of these are beyond mile 11.

If you continue, you'll find another old boxcar at mile 16, still sporting its original stove; you're also likely to see clusters of whitewater rafters. To allow rafters a quiet float, powerboats are allowed on the river only every other week. (If you plan to need a rescue, pick their week.) Washouts make the trail impassable beyond mile 18.5.

When you're ready, turn around and return the way you came.

34 Lake Wallula Scenic River Hiking Trail (Hat Rock Scenic Corridor)

Umatilla, Oregon, is a rural desert community at the southern tip of the I–82 bridge across the Columbia River. It connects the Yakima Valley wine country of Washington to Oregon. The historic trail begins and ends at riverside parks.

Activities:

Location: Umatilla County, 3 miles from the town of Umatilla

Length: 4.9 miles

Surface: Gravel

Wheelchair access: The trail is not wheelchair accessible.

Difficulty: Easy to difficult. Most of the trail is easy; its middle section has some hills and a washout.

Food: You'll find convenience stores and a cafe at Hat Rock State Park; there are mini marts 1.1 miles west of McNary Beach Park. The town of Umatilla is 3 miles from McNary Beach Park.

Rest rooms: There are flush toilets and drinking water at both parks from May through September; a chemical toilet is available year-round at McNary Beach Park.

Seasons: The trail can be used year-round.

Access and parking: To begin at the western trailhead, drive 3 miles east of Umatilla on Route 730 to the MCNARY PARK sign. Turn north (left) onto Port of Umatilla Road and drive 1 mile to the McNary Beach Park Recreation Area entrance.

The entrance to Hat Rock State Park, the trail's eastern terminus, is 8.2 miles east of Umatilla on Route 730.

Rentals: No rentals are available along this trail.

Contacts:
- McNary Dam Natural Resources, (541) 922–2226
- Hat Rock State Park, (541) 567–5032 or 567–4188

Bus routes: None

The Hat Rock Scenic Corridor is a chunk of rugged riverside perched on a bank above the Columbia River in the Oregon desert. Ride or walk this trail on a sunny day—and most days here are sunny—and you'll know you're in heaven. The trail is hot and unshaded, however; bring water, serious sunscreen, and a hat.

McNary Beach Park, on the western end, lies adjacent to the dam that in 1953 flooded miles of Oregon-Washington Railroad and Navigation Company (OWR&N) line and several towns upriver. The Mc-Nary Dam was built to produce hydroelectric power and to relieve the problems of navigating the Columbia. Inland waterways were critical to trade, and the Umatilla rapids caused more grief and delay to barge lines than any other obstacle on the Columbia River. The dam flooded the main-line railroad from Cold Springs to Attalia

Hat Rock looms over the trail.

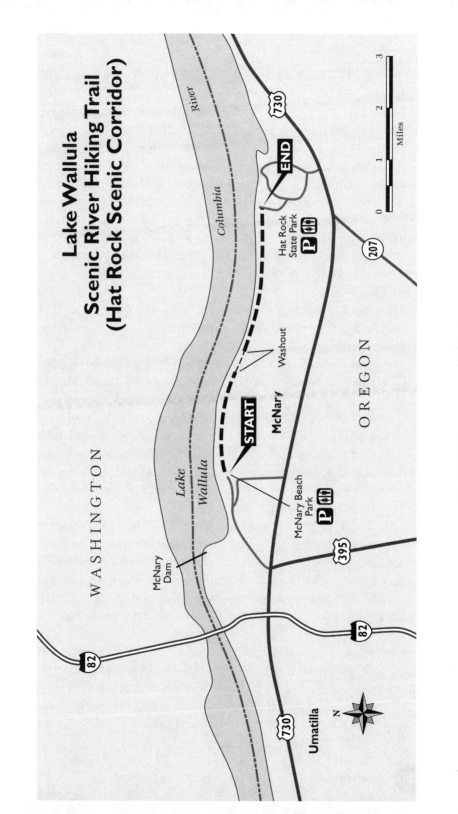

and Wallula. The 35-mile backflow, along the Yakima line to the Kalan Bridge, was called Lake Wallula.

Following dam construction, the towns and railyards were moved to their new location and the railroad rebuilt. This boosted the success of the OWR&N, an operating segment of the Union Pacific Railroad. Though the waterways could now compete with the rails, government funding allowed the railroad to improve the tracks that had been so hastily blasted through basalt cliffs in 1880. Sharp curves, rockfall, and avalanches had for decades caused delays and derailments, shoving engines over the banks and into the river.

The last steam-powered train ran these tracks in 1955. Now you can walk 4.9 miles of the route beside the chunk of history that lies under Lake Wallula.

The paved access to the trail starts to the left off the park road before you reach the parking lot. It quickly becomes dirt and gravel as it cuts into the basalt cliffs and through the sagebrush.

The grassy riverfront at McNary Beach Park has a fishing dock and picnic tables. Look for the trail at the east end of the parking lot. The first mile is easy. Then the trail climbs up onto a steeper riverbank with great views. Choose the uphill fork where a side trail heads down to a pump plant. The trail seems to end at a washout 2 miles down the trail, but you can climb up and over a narrow, rocky segment to continue. Use caution. The bank is undercut and drops into the river far below. If you find it too risky, explore the east end of the trail from Hat Rock State Park.

As you approach Hat Rock State Park, the trail becomes relatively flat. The view becomes more interesting, as homes, inlets, and rock formations appear. The scenery changes as the land creeps into the river and the basalt cliffs change shape. The river is wide and blue, the sagebrush a faded yellow. Boats cruise by and locals walk their dogs and themselves down the trail. Listen for the metallic rustle of the cheatgrass and bunchgrass in the wind.

Arriving at Hat Rock State Park is like entering the Emerald City. The desert browns and yellows turn into bright green. Everything takes on color and texture and life. Green grass, green willow trees, and flowers encircle the pond, where ducks and geese create ripples as they fetch gifts of food. Anglers wait on the banks of the inlet and

- Pacific Salmon Visitors Information Center, (541) 922–4388)
- The town of McNary, (541) 922–3211
- Umatilla Marina Park, (541) 567–5032
- McNary Wildlife Nature Area, (541) 922–3211

pond for steelhead, bass, or catfish. A little bridge across the inlet leads you to the open desert trails. The Hat Rock towers above the park looking like . . . you guessed it, a huge hat.

The donors of the parkland, the Jewett family, maintain this lovely park and pond and the trails out of appreciation for its special beauty.

This neighborhood is popular for golf and, across the river, for wine tasting. See Trail 27 for information on wineries and events thirty minutes from Umatilla. And 1.1 mile west of McNary Beach on Willamette Avenue, you'll find the Desert River Inn and golf course, a tavern, and a convenience store.

When you're ready, turn around and return the way you came.

OC&E–Woods Line State Trail
by Klamath Rails-to-Trails Group

Explore the 98-mile OC&E–Woods Line State Trail for its soli-
tude and panoramic views. Walkers, joggers, cyclists, equestrians, skateboarders, and other nonmotorized travelers have one
thing in common on this great pathway—they're all welcome!

Activities:

Location: OC&E Main Line: Klamath Falls to Bly, in Klamath County. Woods
Line: Beatty to the Thompson Reservoir, Klamath County.

Length: 98 miles (63 miles on the OC&E Main Line Trail; 35 miles on the
Woods Line Trail)

Surface: The trail is paved for 3.3 miles out of Klamath Falls. On the remainder of the trail, all the heavy ballast has been graded off and compacted
with a vibrating roller to create a smooth surface. Equestrians and joggers
share a wood-chip trail.

Wheelchair access: Only the paved section is wheelchair accessible.

Difficulty: Easy to moderate

Food: Klamath Falls has all services. There are convenience stores in Olene,
Dairy, Sprague River, Beatty, and Bly; cafes in Dairy, Sprague River, Beatty,
and Bly.

Rest rooms: There are rest rooms at the Route 39 Trailhead at Wiard Park,
and at Horse Glade Trailhead.

Seasons: The trail can be used year-round.

Access and parking:
- *Route 140 (three trailheads):* Reach Klamath Falls from I–97 or Route 39 to
  Route 140. Drive 0.25 mile east of Washburn Way on Crosby Avenue for
  the Crosby Trailhead in Klamath Falls. Turn left between the self-storage
  facility and Circle DE Lumber. The Route 39 Trailhead is 0.4 mile south
  of South Sixth Street; the Dairy Y Trailhead is 0.9 mile north of Dairy.
- *Switchback Trailhead:* Continue 3 miles north of Dairy and turn left onto
  Squaw Flat Road. Turn left onto U.S. Forest Service Road 22 at 12 miles.
  This is the trailhead to use for cross-country skiing.
- *Sycan Siding Trailhead:* This trailhead lies at the intersection of the OC&E
  Trail and the Woods Line Trail. To reach it, take Route 140 to Beatty. Turn
  left onto Godowa Springs Road. After 2.1 miles, turn right onto Sycan Road.

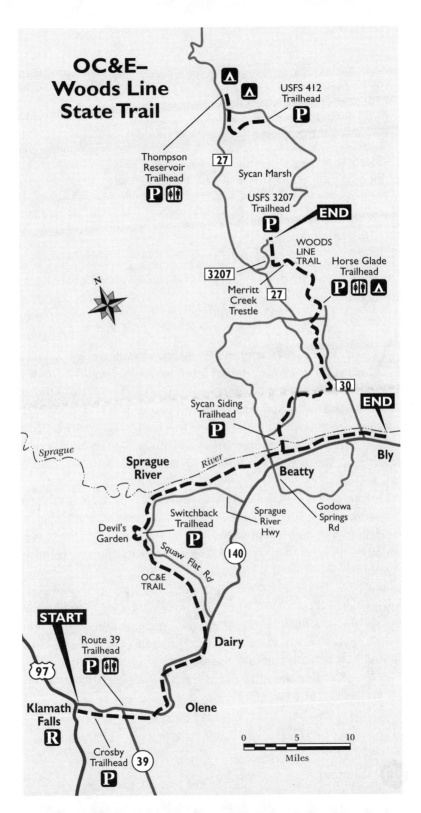

OC&E–
Woods Line
State Trail

Thompson
Reservoir
Trailhead

USFS 412
Trailhead

[27]

Sycan Marsh

USFS 3207
Trailhead

END

WOODS
LINE
TRAIL

Horse Glade
Trailhead

[3207]

Merritt
Creek
Trestle

[27]

[30]

END

Sycan Siding
Trailhead

Sprague
River

Sprague   River

Beatty

Bly

Godowa
Springs
Rd

Switchback
Trailhead

Sprague
River
Hwy

Devil's
Garden

Squaw Flat Rd

[140]

OC&E
TRAIL

START

Route 39
Trailhead

Dairy

[97]

Klamath
Falls

[R]

Olene

Crosby
Trailhead

[39]

0   5   10
Miles

N

Where the paved road turns to dirt, turn right again. Park at the yellow railroad snowplow.

- *Horse Glade Trailhead:* Take Route 140 east from Beatty for 15 miles, to Ivory Pine Road. Turn north and drive 12.5 miles. Turn left onto Forest Road 27 toward Thompson Reservoir and continue 1.3 miles.
- *Forest Road 3207 Trailhead:* This trailhead places you at the north end of the developed trail. Continue 9.7 miles farther on Forest Road 27, turn right onto Forest Road 3207, and park along the railbed.
- *Thompson Reservoir Trailhead:* Continue for 30.2 miles on Forest Road 27.

Rentals: Yankee Peddler Bicycles, 2616 Altamont Drive, Klamath Falls, (541) 850–2453.

Contacts:
- Collier State Park, (541) 783-2471, www.oregonstateparks.org/park_230.php
- Klamath Rails-to-Trails Group, (541) 884–3050, www.klamath-trails.org

Bus routes: None

• •

A t the turn of the twentieth century, railroads were leading the growth of the West. Robert Strahorn had a dream of connecting central and eastern Oregon with rail lines by linking Klamath Falls to Lakeview via Sprague River, and Bend and Burns via Sprague River and Silver Lake. The first step in this grand plan was the OC&E, also known as the Klamath Municipal Railway. Groundbreaking occurred near Third Street and Klamath Avenue in Klamath Falls on July 3, 1917.

Quickly a ribbon of steel stretched out toward Sprague River. Soon mills and branch lines sprang up along this new railway. The line was declared open on September 16, 1923. In 1927 the line was extended to Bly, but that would be the end of the line for Strahorn's dream.

Southern Pacific and Great Northern (later Burlington Northern) jointly operated the OC&E from 1925 until 1974. One railroad would manage the line for five years then pass responsibility to the other for five years. Weyerhauser took over the entire line in 1974, but by the end of the 1980s the line was no longer a cost-effective way to move logs. The line was rail-banked and handed over to Oregon Parks and Recreation in 1992.

The trail is actually two trails—the original OC&E, and the old Weyerhauser Woods Line that heads from Beatty to just north of the Sycan Marsh. The Woods Line heads uphill from south to north and is forested with sagebrush meadows. On the main-line trail, you'll travel through ranchland and desert, with one hilly section.

If you're a cross-country ski enthusiast, snow can be found in the switchback area and on miles 10 through 30.5 of the Woods Line, though trailheads are not cleared of snow for parking.

OC&E Main Line Trail, 63 miles

The first 3.3 miles of the OC&E Trail are paved, starting at Washburn Way in Klamath Falls and ending at Route 39. Pass by local shopping areas and through residential neighborhoods. This section receives the most use, but there's much more to explore as the trail heads east.

The trail passes through agricultural areas with wonderful views of surrounding mountains, including Mount Shasta to the south. The trail crosses Route 140 and pushes on through juniper and sagebrush to the town of Olene, and then the Poe Valley. To your right spreads a panoramic view of the Poe Valley and the Lost River.

The Merritt Creek Trestle. (Courtesy Art Sevigny)

The trail continues on to Swede's Cut, the spot where Swedish workers carved a pass through solid rock to gain access to Pine Flat. The job required great skill at using drills and black powder and more than a bit of bravado.

Emerge from Pine Flat at the town of Dairy at mile 18. To visit the small tavern, cafe, or convenience store in town, continue to the Dairy Siding just east of town. Bear right. Continue to the T-intersection with Route 140 and turn right; Dairy is 0.8 mile away. This is your last chance for food or water until the town of Sprague River at mile 35. The valleys around Dairy and Bonanza saw violent conflicts between Native Americans and settlers during the Modoc Indian War in 1872.

The trail heads north from Dairy to skirt around Bly Mountain via Switchback Hill. Just past Hildebrand the forested trail gains 600 feet in 9 miles at a 2 percent grade. Climb up Switchback Hill on a large horseshoe turn, so sharp that the end of the train saw the lead cars passing directly above. The switchback allowed the heavy trains laden with timber and some cattle to make the 600-foot climb. Passengers rode the line only in the 1920s. The tracks zigzag over the steep hillside, forming a double switchback. There were once plans to cut a tunnel through Bly Mountain to replace the switchbacks, but they never materialized.

From the top, look to the southeast for a great view of the Devil's Garden. Take a 7-mile (round trip) side trip to this volcanic caldera on old logging roads.

The trail descends to the river and the town of Sprague River at mile 38.5. Here in the Sprague River Valley you'll find country stores and small cafes, vistas of surrounding mountains, forests, and ranches. Your next stop is Beatty, at mile 51.5. To reach this town, take Godowa Springs Road about a mile south to Route 140.

Just east of Beatty, the Woods Line branches north. To continue on the main trail, head east through pastures of grazing cattle and marshy and open-water areas. Sandhill cranes, eagles, red-tailed hawks, egrets, great blue herons, ducks and geese, swarms of red-winged blackbirds, beavers, deer, and other wildlife can be seen along the Sprague River. The trail ends in Bly near the South Fork of the Sprague River and just southwest of the Gearhart Wilderness Area (America's least used wilderness), at mile 63.25.

Five-Mile Creek. (Courtesy Art Sevigny)

Woods Line Trail, 35 miles

To take the Woods Line Trail, head northeast from Beatty on a steady
uphill climb. The trail crosses over the Sprague River and passes by
the Sycan Shops (former maintenance yard for the Woods Line).
Keep an eye out for an old tipple hidden in the woods. The trestle
at mile 9 was abandoned once the ravine was filled in. At mile 10
you'll reach Five-Mile Creek and trout fishing; for the next 6 miles,
this creek will be your companion. Arrive at Horse Glade Trailhead
at mile 18.75. Here you'll find a rest room and camping. Pass through
second-growth forest; at mile 27 you'll cross the most spectacular
structure on the trail: the Merritt Creek Trestle, which spans 400 feet
and rises 100 feet above the ground.

At present the trail ends 5 miles to the north at the Sycan Marsh,
then starts again just north of the marsh. It continues for 4 miles
through the Thompson Valley, ending at the old 500 Load Area (a
log loading area) just south of the Thompson Reservoir (camping,
water, boating, and rest rooms are available). For a one-way shuttle
trip that's all downhill, park one car at one of the northern trailheads
and another at Sycan Siding.

The trail is scheduled to be paved a total of 8 miles out of Klamath Falls in the summer of 2002. The U.S. Forest Service hopes to eliminate the gap at the Sycan Marsh as well.

Other future plans include the addition of rest rooms and water at existing trailheads; campsites at Dairy, Switchback, Beatty, and Bly; the development of other trailheads, benches, and interpretive signs; and the clearing of snow from trailheads for cross-country skiing.

The Klamath Rails-to-Trails Group would like to wish you many happy trails!

MORE RAIL-TRAILS

N Malheur Rail Trail

The Malheur National Forest sits in the Blue Mountains of eastern Oregon. It's hot in summer and snowy in winter. The Malheur Rail Trail is a somewhat rugged trail that travels through a draw. The forest service has rated it difficult due to its surface; its grade is mostly moderate.

Activities:

Location: Malheur National Forest, John Day, Grant County

Length: 12.5 miles

Surface: Ballast

Wheelchair access: The trail is not wheelchair accessible.

Difficulty: Difficult

Food: No food is available along this trail.

Rest rooms: There are rest rooms at the trailhead on Forest Road 1600097, but no drinking water.

Seasons: The trail can be used year-round, though it's difficult to access in winter.

Access and parking: From Prairie City, take Route 62 for 19 miles to Summit Prairie. From here, travel west on U.S. Forest Service Road 16 to Forest Road 1600133. You'll find the trailhead at the junction with Forest Road 1600097.

Rentals: No rentals are available along this trail.

Contact: U.S. Forest Service at Wind River Ranger Station, (541) 820–3800, www.fs.fed.us/r6/malheur/frmain.htm

Bus routes: None

Mill City Trail

The trail begins on a refurbished railroad bridge that crosses the salmon-filled pool created by Mill City Falls. It parallels the river for a while and offers several scenic points.

Activities:

Location: Beaverton, Linn County

Length: 1.5 miles

Surface: Asphalt with some packed gravel

Wheelchair access: The trail is not wheelchair accessible.

Difficulty: Easy.

Food: There are restaurants near the start of the trail in Mill City.

Rest rooms: There are no rest rooms along the trail.

Seasons: The trail can be used year-round.

Access and parking: Take Route 22E to Mill City. Turn right onto Northeast Second Avenue, then turn left at the T-intersection with Wall Street to reach the Sennium River. You'll see the railroad bridge on your right beyond the parking area. Park and cross the street to the river.

Rentals: No rentals are available along this trail.

Contact: City of Mill City, (503) 897–2302

Bus routes: None

Oregon Electric ROW Trail and Linear Park

This short trail connects two parks in a rural section of Beaverton. It's part of a master plan to link Beaverton's 55 square miles of parks with a pedestrian and recreation path.

Activities:

Location: Beaverton, Washington County

Length: 1 mile

Surface: Asphalt

Wheelchair access: The entire trail is wheelchair accessible.

Difficulty: Easy

Food: No food is available along this trail.

Rest rooms: There are no rest rooms along the trail.

Seasons: The trail can be used year-round.

Access and parking: Take Sunset Highway (Route 26) west to Route 217. Turn south, drive to Allen Boulevard, then turn east. At Scholls Ferry Road, turn south. You'll find the west trailhead at the intersection of 92nd Avenue Southwest.

Rentals: No rentals are available along this trail.

Contact: Tualatin Hills Park and Recreation Department, (503) 645–6433

Bus routes: None

Ⓠ Sumpter Valley Interpretive Trail

This interpretive trail marks the highest point of the Sumpter Valley Railway: 5,277 feet. It overlooks switchbacks into the John Day Valley. Learn about the historic railway and why the route was abandoned.

Activities:

Location: Malheur National Forest, John Day, Grant County

Length: 0.25 mile

Surface: Asphalt

Wheelchair access: The entire trail is wheelchair accessible but watch areas with steep terrain.

Difficulty: Moderate

Food: No food is available along this trail.

Rest rooms: There are no rest rooms along the trail.

Seasons: While the trail can be used year-round, the lot adjacent to the highway isn't plowed; expect snow from November through April.

Access and parking: From Prairie City, take County Road 26 for 8 miles. The trail is located before Dixie Summit on the right.

Rentals: No rentals are available along this trail.

Contact: Malheur National Forest, (541) 820–3800, www.fs.fed.us/r6/malheur/

Bus routes: None

Appendix A

RENTAL INFORMATION

Puget Sound

Bicycles

Al Young Bike and Ski
3615 NE 45th Street
Seattle 98105
(206) 524-2642

Alpine Hut
2215 15th West
Seattle 98119
(206) 284-3575

Bicycle Center
4529 Sandpoint Way NE
Seattle 98105
(206) 523-8300

Blazing Saddles
1230 Western Avenue
Seattle 98101
(206) 341-9994
www.blazingsaddles.com

Gregg's Greenlake Cycle
7007 Woodlawn Avenue NE
Seattle 98115
(206) 523-1822

Montlake Bicycle Shop
2223 24th Avenue E
Seattle   98112
(206) 329-7333

R&E Cycles
5627 University Way NE
Seattle 98105
(206) 527-4822
www.rodcycle.com

Ti Cycles—demos only
(behind University Village)
2943 NE Blakely Street
Seattle 98105
(206) 522-7602

Skates

Al Young Bike and Ski
3615 NE 45th Street
Seattle 98105
(206) 524-2642

Alpine Hut
2215 15th West
Seattle 98119
(206) 284-3575

Fiorini Sports
4720 University Place NE
Seattle 98105
(206) 523-9610
www.fiorinisports.com

The Good Sport
10700 5th Avenue, NE
Seattle 98125
(206) 526-8087
www.goodsport.net

Gregg's Greenlake Cycle
7007 Woodlawn Avenue NE
Seattle 98115
(206) 523-1822

Urban Surf
2100 N. Northlake Way
Seattle 98103
(206) 545-9463

East Side of Lake Washington

Bicycles
Bothell Ski and Bike
17816 NE Bothell Way
Bothell 98011
(425) 286–3747
www.bikesale.com

Montlake Bicycle Shop
211 Kirkland Avenue
Kirkland 98033
(425) 828–3800

Montlake Bicycle Shop
10 103rd Avenue NE
Bellevue 98004
(425) 462–8823

Redmond Cycle
16205 Redmond Way
Redmond 98052
(425) 885–6363

Sammamish Valley Cycle
8451 164th Avenue NE
Redmond 98052
(425) 881–8442

Skates
Play it Again Sports
17622 108th SE
Renton 98055
(425) 227–8777

Northwestern Washington

Skates
Play it Again Sports
19513 Highway 99
Lynnwood 98036
(425) 670–1184

Cross Country Skis and Snowshoes
Backpacker's Supply
5206 South Tacoma Way
Tacoma 98409
(253) 472–4402

Marmot Mountain Works
827 Bellevue Way NE
Bellevue 98004
(425) 453–1515

REI
222 Yale Avenue
Seattle 98109
(206) 470–4020

Wilderness Sports
14340 NE 20th Street
Bellevue 98007
(425) 746–0500

In-line Skating Instruction
Get Your Bearings In-line Skate
   School
(206) 283–0575

Nordic Way Ski and In-line Skate
   School
(425) 391–2781

Skateability
(206) 227–6868

Skiing Instruction
Nordic Way Ski and In-line Skate
   School
(425) 391–2781

The Summit at Snoqualmie
(425) 434–7669

Appendix B

ORGANIZATIONS FOR ADVOCACY, EDUCATION, AND INFORMATION

Adventure Cycling Association
P.O. Box 8308
Missoula, MT 59807–8308
(406) 721–1776
www.adv-cycling.org

BBTC (Backcounty Bicycle Trails
  Club)
P.O. Box 21288
Seattle, WA 98111–3288
(206) 283–2995

Bicycle Alliance of Washington
903 Union Street #100
Seattle, WA 98101–1911
www.bikealliance.org

Bike Works
3709 S. Ferdinand Street
Seattle, WA 98118
(206) 725–9408
www.scn.org/bikeworks

Cascade Bicycle Club
P.O. Box 15165
Seattle, WA 98115
www.cascade.org

International In-line Skate
  Association (IISA)
105 South 7th Street
Wilmington, NC 28401
(910) 762–7004
www.iisa.org

League of American Bicyclists
1612 K Street, NW #104
Washington, D.C. 20006
(202) 822–1333
www.bikeleague.org

Spokane Bicycle Club
P.O. Box 62
Spokane, WA 99210–0062
(509) 325–1171

Tri–City Bicycle Club
P.O. Box 475
Richmond, WA 99352

Washington In-line Skate
  Association (WILSA)
www.wilsa.org

Get Your Rail-Trail Guidebooks

- Florida   • California
- **New England States** (CT, RI,VT, MA, ME, NH)
- **Mid-Atlantic States** (MD, DE, VA, WV)

Additional states coming soon - check availability in Fall 2001 at www.railtrails.org or in our quarterly magazine *Rails to Trails*.

Guidebooks Feature:
- ✓ Top Trails
- ✓ Maps
- ✓ Photos
- ✓ Detailed Narratives

"An invaluable guidebook to some of the country's best rail-trails....quick and easy-to-read details, get us on the trail fast, while the historical mentions add spark."

Linda Frahm
Walking Magazine

3 Easy Ways to Order:

1. Mail form on the next page with your check or credit card information.

2. Call 1-800-888-7747, ext 11 with your Visa, MasterCard or American Express card.

3. Visit www.railtrails.org in Fall 2001 to order online.

Please send me the following RTC Guidebooks!

❏ **Mid Atlantic States** (MD, DE, VA, WV)   ❏ **California**
❏ **New England States** (CT, RI, VT, MA, NH, ME)   ❏ **Florida**

Item #	Guidebooks	Member Price	Non-Member Price	Qty	Total
GPG1	Mid-Atlantic	$12.95	$14.95		$
GPG2	New England	$12.95	$14.95		
GPG3	California	$12.95	$14.95		
GPG4	Florida	$10.95	$12.95		
			Order Total	$	
		Sales Tax (CA, FL, MA, MI, OH, PA)	$		
			Handling Charge	$ 4.95	
			Total Enclosed	$	

❏   I want to join Rails-to-Trails Conservancy. My membership contribution is enclosed (amount checked below). Send me my member packet including my *Sampler of America's Rail-Trails* and one year of *Rails to Trails*, the colorful, quarterly magazine that celebrates trails and greenways. I will also receive discounts on publications and merchandise.

❏ **$18 Regular**   ❏ **$50 Patron**
❏ **$75 Benefactor**   ❏ **$1000 - Trailblazer Society level includes
                              invitations to exclusive rail-trail excursions.**

❏ My check, payable to Rails-to-Trails Conservancy, is enclosed.

❏ Charge my Credit Card   ❏ MC ❏ VISA ❏ American Express

Card #_____ Exp._____

Signature_____

Name on card (Please Print)_____

Ship to: (Please Print)

Name_____

⸱et_____

⸱ate, Zip_____

)_____

       ⸱s_____